M.A. HUGHES

never too late to tell

A Memoir

the kind press

Copyright © 2021 Margaret Hughes

First published by the kind press, 2021

All rights reserved. No part of this book may be reproduced, stored in a retrieval system or transmitted in any form or by any means, electronic, mechanical photocopying, recording or otherwise, without written permission from the author and publisher. This book is memoir. It reflects the author's present recollections of experiences over time. Some names and characteristics have been changed, some events have been compressed, and some dialogue has been recreated.

This publication contains the opinions and ideas of its author. It is intended to provide helpful and informative material on the subjects addressed in the publication. While the publisher and author have used their best efforts in preparing this book, the material in this book is of the nature of general comment only.

Cataloguing-in-Publication entry is available from the National Library Australia.

ISBN: 978-0-6450887-2-4
ISBN: 978-0-6450887-3-1 (ebook)

Cover design by Mila Book Covers
Typeset by Nicola Matthews, Nikki Jane Design

Dedicated to Robert William Edward – Robbie
For: James Llewellyn, Megan Elizabeth and Rob's Friends

Proverbs 10:7
The memory of the just is blessed.

And on my way home I had, for the first time in my life, a conviction—I mean not a thought but knowledge—that life can't possibly end at death. I had the punctuation wrong. I thought it was a full stop, but it's only a comma, or a dash— or better still, a colon: I don't believe in heaven or hell, or punishment or reward, or the survival of the ego; but what about energy, spirit, soul, imagination, love? The force for which we have no word? How preposterous, to think that it could die!

— Helen Garner, True Stories: The Collected Short Non-Fiction, (Text, 2017)

Contents

	Prologue	ix
1	I Need to Tell You	1
2	Is This a Bad Dream?	9
3	Taking a Year Off	13
4	Kindness and Hospitality Everywhere	17
5	Adapting to Changes	25
6	A Friendship Develops	33
7	Together in The Middle East	43
8	Romantic Beirut	49
9	Separated	55
10	At the Kibbutz	59
11	Your Beginning Revealed	65
12	Back to England	75
13	Amazingly Reunited	79
14	In the Caravan	85
15	Making the Right Decision	91
16	What Is Best for You?	95
17	Your Arrival	99
18	A Family	105
19	Settling In	109

20	Christmas in Cornwall	111
21	Popular in Paris	115
22	A Melbourne Welcome	119
23	A Baby Brother	125
24	Life in The Suburbs	129
25	Townsville and a Baby Sister	133
26	Life in Bulldust	139
27	South Africa	149
28	Brisbane Then Eimeo	161
29	1 Sunset Boulevarde	167
30	Scone in The Hunter Valley	175
31	Unravelling in Sydney	185
32	Bereft but Not Broken	193
33	You Are the Best Thing	207
34	Surreal Days	213
35	Your Inclusive Nature	223
	May 2, 2021	*227*
	Acknowledgements	*240*
	About the Author	*241*

Prologue

At Wandiligong, Autumn 2019

I'm gazing north up the Wandiligong valley. Autumn is entering the garden and spreading to the hills beyond. The golden ash was the first to suddenly change—green one minute, exploding yellow the next.

Nearer to the house, the claret ash is burgundy on the tips stretching up and up, and just beyond the deck, the red oak has crimson tints reaching outwards from the centre. The extraordinary breadth of this sprawling oak can only be appreciated by standing underneath it and looking up through the vast canopy.

Remember, Robbie, how I told you that they were all planted when I was at school? Grandpa, who planted them, would be amazed at their size.

Back when we only came to Wandi in the school holidays, gathering hazelnuts at Easter was a family ritual. You, with Jamie, Megan, Grandpa and I, would crawl around under the outspread branches, plopping the brown shiny hazelnuts into plastic buckets, and picking out those that had fallen in between the coppiced trunks.

Right now, I'm on a break from crawling under the trees and gathering the last of this year's crop. I've made a pot of tea and carried it out onto the deck, then plonked down on floral cushions in a big metal armchair.

You didn't know this deck, Robbie, on the western side of my new house, a plain rectangle I designed and built on a strict budget. After all the different houses we'd lived in, I tried to incorporate features that are important to me, but I wish Garth—with his civil engineering design experience—had been here to advise. It's well-insulated and the windows are double-glazed.

It surprised me that so many decisions were necessary for building a simple house. The strict fire overlay required steel window frames, not timber, and no louvre windows because the house is so close to the bush. It is small enough to be comfortable for just me, but roomy enough for visitors too. The floors are made of a light, honey-coloured local timber, Mount Beauty ash. It was a relief to move here after all those years spent in that rambling two-storey house in Wahroonga, with its eight external doors. There are only three doors to lock here, and they often remain unlocked.

We all loved reading at Wandi. The Easter we shared JRR Tolkien's *The Lord of the Rings*, you were in Year 8. I was halfway through reading it, but because it was a paperback copy, I tore it in half and continued reading the second half while you started at the beginning. Jamie and Megan kept yelling at you to come outside to play. 'I'll just finish this page,' you'd call back. 'After this chapter,' you'd say.

You, Jamie, Megan and I played Scrabble at night and argued about the spelling of words without consulting a dictionary. "Ax" I insisted was a legitimate word, but you wanted it to be "axe". We were both competitive, but you usually won with your superior vocabulary, being better at English than I ever was. Grandma would glance up from reading the paper, amused by our wrangling. Grandpa snoozed by the fire.

Today, on my hands and knees, tossing hazelnuts into a tin bucket, I think of the last time you were here. I look at the photo of you lying in front of the smoky fire, with Megan combing your hair which was thick and long and the colour of straw. It was Easter 1991. You no longer had to follow school rules about appearance and you cut it yourself. We laughed at how it stuck straight up in front.

Jamie was in the Knox Firsts Rugby Squad, so wasn't at Wandi because he was at a training camp near Gosford. So, it was just Grandma, Grandpa, you, Megan and me. Grandma and I did the cooking while you and Megan did the dishes. You drove Megan and me for eight hours from Sydney, and the next day, much to Grandma's delight, you drove us to the shops in Bright. I enjoyed being a passenger after so many years of being the only driver. Grandma and I chatted, relaxed, and enjoyed cappuccinos at a cafe.

Today, under the old pear tree, bright yellow crocuses are flowering over my childhood pet dog Rusty's grave. I've always liked autumn the best, but I am looking forward to winter too, when the snow will be heavy on Mount Hotham and Falls Creek and will sprinkle over the nearby hills, and when a persistent chill in the air calls for the combustion wood fire to burn non-stop.

There are days when the sun will shine brightly in a blue sky, but I know that the frost preceding those days can kill overnight, just like it did my thriving lime tree when it was laden with perfect, green, thin-skinned juicy fruit last winter. My vegetable garden, bursting with lettuce, red cabbage for sauerkraut, kale and spring onions, is netted against the pesky parrots.

Through every window I can look out at trees, grass and garden, and feel grateful to be here. This land has been a compass point in our lives.

I think of your last night at the old weekender, when that photo was taken of you sitting in front of the smoky fire. I think how wonderful it would be if we could play Scrabble or share a book in front of my new fire that doesn't billow smoke into the room.

But that is not to be.

1

I Need to Tell You

I need to tell you, Robbie, you were amazing from the moment you were born. Even before you emerged into this world, you taught me so much.

As a teenager, your strength kept your siblings and me together after your dad left. I am in awe of what you did. Initially, your departure threatened to open up another gap in our family, but you continue to be acknowledged by Jamie, Megan and me. We reminisce about how special you were and we smile about times when you made us laugh. Thus, you are here with us, still making us laugh. Palpably alive. Too unique to be gone.

I know you didn't mean to leave us so suddenly. Your friend's shaky voice on the phone, the shocking news, left me numb and disbelieving. You calculated risks before taking them, so how could this be fatal? You had defied odds often and emerged unscathed. You, who would never have deliberately caused anyone pain. After quickly adjusting to your dad's leaving, your lifestyle had continued as a happy, fruitful, fulfilling one. On that pivotal day, 2 May 1991, many lives were changed. Robbie, it unfolded for me like this.

* * *

'The body must be identified tonight.' The policeman's voice over the phone sounded harsh, uncompromising to my confused, disbelieving brain.

'Tonight?' I replied. 'I don't think I can manage it tonight. It's too hard. It's too soon, and I have other children to look after. We're all in shock. Can't it wait until tomorrow?'

'No, it must be tonight. Can someone else do it instead of you?'

'No, there is no-one else.'

Of course, it had to be me. But, The Rocks is such a long way from Wahroonga. I had no strength, and I felt numb. And what about Megan and Jamie? Who would look after them while I was gone? They were old enough to be left at home, but they were struggling with the impact of this shock, quiet one minute, sobbing the next. They couldn't be left alone.

I rang my friend, Beverley, whose prayers had helped me through some traumatic challenges before. I knew no-one and nothing could help the children and me more now.

* * *

Thursday 2 May 1991 began as an unexceptional day. I brought in our bins. I chatted to a neighbour who was taking hers in, still dressed in her nightie. I took Buster to the local park and walked down a fire trail, both of us greeting the usual morning dog walkers. I vacuumed upstairs and prepared some sourdough to bake the next day. There was an unusually difficult phone conversation with Grandma. She wanted to sell and move up from Melbourne to Sydney to be closer to me and her adored grandchildren. But Grandpa did not welcome change. He no longer even wanted to go to the farm at Wandiligong. It was sad to hear the hint of desperation in her voice, and I hung up wondering when I could help her. Maybe in the next school holidays, I thought.

In the afternoon, I was digging out onion weed from around the standard apricot-coloured floribunda roses when I noticed the new dark blue pair of jeans I'd bought you, still pegged up after three days on the line.

'When will you wear them?' I had asked you the day before.

'They at least have to be faded,' you'd said. 'I'd cut holes in them too, Mum, but you probably wouldn't like that.'

I heard the phone ringing. I rushed inside to the sound of our grandfather clock chiming four. I picked up the receiver and strained to hear a voice so soft and shaky that I didn't immediately recognise it.

'Hullo, Mrs Hughes, it's Rob's friend, Richard. There's been an accident. Rob's been in an accident.'

'Where are you ringing from, Richard?' My voice was normal, matter-of-fact. It couldn't be serious. You had always come home despite your sometimes risky behaviour in the past. You were settled now, happy in the present and with future plans.

'Milsons Point Station, the station on top of the bridge.' His voice was trembling.

A few minutes later he rang again, his voice almost inaudible. 'They've carried Rob out of the tunnel on a stretcher, covered up,' he said. 'I think Rob is dead.'

That's impossible, I thought. It was maybe an hour later when I heard the doorbell ring and reluctantly opened the front door. I faced two police officers, a man and a woman. They were young, solemn, nervous. One of them started to speak but I interrupted.

'I know about my son,' I said, softly.

'How did you find out?' the woman said.

'Rob's friend phoned me from Milsons Point Station. He didn't give me any details about what happened.'

'There'll be an investigation, but it should have been us who told you,' the man said. 'We're very sorry.' I watched them turn and walk away slowly down the front path through the mandarin tree hedge.

I could hear Megan in the kitchen, home from school. There was no easy way to say it. I got the words out and she burst into tears. The next moment she was crying hysterically. She asked me where Jamie was. I told her he had stayed at school to do his homework with the boarders and would be home in a few hours. I spoke quietly, not wanting to talk or think.

'I want Jamie here,' she said. 'Can't he come home?'

I buckled to her grief. She desperately needed comforting because you were her closest friend and substitute dad since she was eleven. But I couldn't drive the short distance to Jamie's school, let alone face a classroom. Our beautiful young German neighbour, Silke, was kind. Maybe she'd go? I dragged my feet next door.

'Of course, I'll go to the school and bring Jamie home,' she said.

'Can I go too?' Megan sobbed.

'Yes, but please,' I said to them softly, 'don't tell him anything. Jamie will know something bad has happened. I'd rather tell him when he gets home.'

Silke told me later that when she walked into the classroom of boys doing their homework they all looked up, trying to guess the reason for this rare interruption. Being Year 11 boys, they were probably admiring Silke's beautiful face and model-like figure. She told me that Jamie had asked her if it was about Mum. She had said no, and that's all they had said.

What should I do? I thought. I ought to ring Grandma and Grandpa. This news will crush them. You were their beloved first grandchild and they were so proud of you. No, they could have another sleep without knowing. They'd be expecting a call tomorrow morning anyway because it would be Grandpa's birthday. I'll ring then. Also, I should ring your dad. I called his work number. A colleague told me that Garth was on holiday until next week. No-one in the office knew where he'd gone except that he was camping.

'I'll ring next Monday morning,' I said. 'No, I won't leave a message.' I thought of how Garth had been out of reach on significant occasions early on in our relationship and how it had worked out eventually. There was too much to do now without worrying about how to contact him before Monday.

Tomorrow I would ring my brother Bill in Queensland, and Betsy, my best friend from school in Melbourne. I knew they would be quiet and respectful, supportive. I needed their help.

When the children returned together, I sat with them quietly. I told Jamie that his beloved brother had been killed this afternoon on his way home from uni. Jamie sat down. His face paled, and tears fell down his cheeks. I thought, Please don't cry. I just want to be quiet. It was dark outside when Beverley returned my call. I listened numbly to her caring, compassionate voice.

'You mustn't go by train or be alone,' she said. She organised for one friend to stay with the children and two others to drive me to The Rocks. Kindness and wisdom had prompted these arrangements, and I was grateful, but all I wanted was to be alone in my thoughts with you, Robbie.

I felt your presence. I longed for you to feel loved and supported. What you were going through was unknown. I hoped it wasn't scary. My love for you at that moment couldn't have been deeper. I was hugging you with all my might.

A little later the front doorbell rang again. I thought it was my chauffeurs, but instead I found two strangers, a young man and a woman. The woman had a notebook and pencil poised for writing. They stared hard at me.

'Yes?' I managed to say.

'We're reporters. We would like to write about the incident on the train this afternoon. What do you have to say about it? Do you blame the railways for still operating the red rattlers with their dangerous wide-open doors?'

'I have nothing to say,' I replied. 'Thank you for your interest. Goodbye.'

They retreated down the path muttering, perhaps cursing, obviously not pleased with my answer. There's no way I could have responded to their questions. I closed the door wearily. Everything felt heavy. I found it hard to think.

It was an effort to act normally on the forty-five-minute drive to the city. My friends wanted to be supportive but didn't know what to say. I found it an effort to speak.

We walked into The Rocks Police Station. The fierce fluorescent lighting hit me as I entered the room, where an officer sat behind a desk, frowning with concentration and tapping persistently at a typewriter. He didn't look up, but with raised eyebrows and a nod, indicated some chairs against the wall.

I sat and waited. For what? Why am I here? Couldn't this have waited until tomorrow? *Tap, tap, clack, tap, tap, tap, clack.* The sounds bounced staccato-like off the walls. The officer's frown deepened as he yanked the paper out of the machine, cast his eyes over it and slipped it into a folder on his desk. Only then did he look straight at me.

He must be speaking, I thought. As if from a great distance, I watch his lips move. He stared at me. I realised I must be giving the answers he wanted. I heard his voice, then mine, but none of it penetrated. I felt no connection to the questions or the answers. What is he asking? What am I answering? Please let me go. I don't want to be here. I don't want to think or talk or be with anyone. Let me out. Let me go. It's horrible, don't speak to me. It's too hard, I can't do it. The brightness in this room bothers me. I want to run out into the dark, to be alone. The streets of The Rocks aren't dark, people are everywhere, but I need to get away from the questions.

I heard the officer clearly say, 'The body isn't ready tonight. You'll have to come back in the morning.'

I stared at him. I felt numb and said nothing.

My chauffeurs apologised that they wouldn't be able to drive me again the next day. They'd booked to start a world cruise that was leaving in the morning. That's all right, I thought. Tomorrow is a long way away. It might not come. I might wake up and find out that this has all been a dream.

I walked inside to find Jamie and Megan snuggled into my friend, Pam, on the couch. They were pale but had stopped crying and looked a little comforted. I hugged them and sent them to bed. As Pam left, I hugged her too.

Then I drifted off to bed. I saw vivid images of our last physical moments together, Robbie. Just that morning at breakfast we had a spontaneous game of who blinks first. As usual my eyelids shut within seconds and I laughed helplessly as I stared at your solemn open-eyed expression. You always won those games. Then I had walked out with you to the carport, where you picked up your old white Peugeot bike and wheeled it through the back gate. I smiled at how tall and strong you looked and how pleased you seemed to be heading off to uni. I thought about how much you were embracing life, revelling in the lifestyle university offered, the concerts, the socialising, the new subjects, the freedom.

As you hopped on your bike, grinning, you looked at me and said, 'I've decided to paint T-shirts to sell.'

I had wondered then what pictures you'd paint, what words you would write. Would they be like your other cartoons? Money was tighter since Garth left us, so I understood your wish to make some.

I watched you pedal away, your unbuttoned flannel shirt billowing out at the sides, on your way to Wahroonga station to catch the train to Redfern.

2

Is This a Bad Dream?

I felt trapped in a dream the next day too. My eyes opened. I checked the time and realised with surprise that I had slept for seven hours, thanks I knew, to my friends' prayers. I felt ready to face the day. Then yesterday's heaviness returned, and it felt permanent. Today I had to look at you, but not as I saw you last. I had to make a second trip to The Rocks Police Station. I would learn just what the Bible expression means to 'gird up your loins'. I needed to pull on every bit of strength and courage from deep within just to be able to go through the motions and do something that had to be done, despite it being the last thing I wanted to do.

Another of my friend's husband, Kevin, drove me to The Rocks. I stayed in my thoughts, continuously reaching out to you. I was grateful to be driven and I thanked Kevin. He said he was glad to do it and didn't chat, which was a relief. There was more traffic than last night. We crawled along behind a line of yellow taxis travelling across the bridge and I thought of the times you'd climbed this arc of steel at night, every detail worked out by you beforehand, thoroughly prepared for any eventuality. You always did your homework before undertaking any of your adventures. I knew this because Jamie had told me how last summer at Warriewood Beach you had scientifically described to him the procedure for jumping off the cliff into the turbulent water below.

There were three specific steps to getting into and then out of the water,

Jamie had said. You had outlined every detail to avoid a dangerous situation. So, wasn't it crazy that a simple movement killed you yesterday?

A younger, much more softly mannered officer met us at the police station. He looked at me kindly and said that he was driving me to the morgue and wondered what my friend would do in the meantime. Kevin said not to worry about him, that he'd wait. In the police car, the officer asked me if I had any questions. My brain wasn't working.

'No, no questions,' I said. But I did wonder what a morgue is like.

The mortician, another youngish man a bit shorter than the policeman and dressed all in white, greeted me formally at the brick entrance to the morgue. He and the policeman seemed to know each other and shook hands. They pointed to a metal door and explained to me that the body was through there, and that identification by me was just a formality.

'Do you understand?' the mortician said. 'It can be quick.'

I understood. I'd seen on television how people identify bodies. The mortician pulls back the cloth covering the body to reveal the face. The witness glances, nods yes or shakes no, and it's all over. The identifier answers, the law is fulfilled. But this was not a television drama. It was real life, mine and yours. The policeman pushed open the heavy inner door and indicated that I should enter. He and the mortician followed me in.

'May I be alone?' I asked. 'I'd like to be alone.'

They looked at each other, scrutinised my face, looked back at each other, and nodded.

'I don't know how long I'll be,' I said.

'Just come out when you're ready,' the policeman said gently, and together they left the room.

I might be a while, I thought, and then I shivered. It was cold. I hesitated before inching towards the stainless steel trolley covered in a white sheet. A long uneven lump bulged along its length. Might there have been a huge mistake and this wasn't you, after all? It couldn't be, could it, because how will I manage without you? Perhaps they'd mixed you up with another teenager's accidental death? It might be someone else. But I must look at what's on the trolley. I slowly pulled the sheet back and uncovered the head.

I stared hard. What was I looking at? There were those features I knew intimately, a face I had loved for eighteen years, thick, tousled straw-hair and eyes wide open. Those eyes transfixed me. How I loved your bright hazel-brown eyes, always twinkling with mirth and intelligence. But those beloved eyes were not there. The eyes in this body were staring, glassy, empty. I tentatively peeled back the sheet to reveal the whole body. The left ankle was swollen where a train had run over it. They'd told me that last night's delay was because when the body was brought out of the tunnel it was black with soot. A mortician attendant had to wash it off. There were still some smudges left. They probably didn't expect me to look at the feet.

I was bewildered by the corpse lying on the trolley and searched for any sign of you, the Robbie I knew. A tall, strong, fit young man's body was stretched out on a trolley. It was your body, but that was not how I held you in my mind. Where was your wit? Where was your love? I couldn't bear the thought of life without you. I knew you wouldn't choose to be here like this.

Then, I heard your voice clearly. 'It's okay, Mum, I haven't left you. I'll always be with you.' Your voice was close, right there, reassuring. You weren't the body on the trolley. We were not separated. I felt glued to the floor, my feet heavy. I wanted to stay. I was glad we were there together, just the two of us.

I had no idea how long I had been in the room, but I also knew I couldn't stay there forever. Reluctantly, I pulled the cloth up and heaved the thick door back open. The two men had been talking in the entrance, and they looked up as I rejoined them.

'Yes,' I said to the mortician, 'the body is my son, Robert.' It was what he needed to hear to get on with his job.

I walked out with the policeman to his car. 'It was so cold in there,' I said.

'Yes,' he replied.

When I returned home from the morgue Jamie and Megan appeared, subdued. I suggested they take Buster for a walk to the park. Pam, who I had known for three years, had kindly come over to be with them again. She sat down with me in the lounge room. Her whole being expressed compassion.

Following my profound experience at the morgue, I felt emotionally safe with her, and said, 'I'd like to explain to you why Rob is so special. There's so much to say. I need to tell Robbie first.'

'Of course, I understand,' Pam said, 'Maybe you'll write it down one day.'

We hugged goodbye, and I watched her car turn onto the road from our circular drive.

I thought about all the things I wished you and I had talked about. Had I made different decisions before and after your birth, the direction of your life would have been profoundly changed. How lucky and blessed I am to have been guided to the right decisions back then. How fortunate for me and others that you were so determined to be born when my pregnancy was unplanned, unexpected.

I had always thought there'd be a good moment to tell you about how you came into being. You have seen the early photos in the family album. I wonder if you ever questioned why there were no photos of your dad and me on our wedding day. I had never talked to you about the circumstances of how your dad and I met. It's still not too late to tell you. I'll tell you now.

First came my decision to leave my job and travel overseas. Some months later Garth and I met in London. You already know some of what I'm going to say next, but not in this context.

3

Taking a Year Off

Robbie, it was 1970. I had taught at a Victorian high school in the Wimmera for three years, then at a Melbourne school for three years while I finished an arts degree at Monash University, part-time. I was feeling restless, so I decided to take twelve months off from teaching, without pay and without plans.

'That was sudden,' a colleague said when the principal announced my decision at a staff meeting. 'What are you going to do?'

'I don't know.' I shrugged. 'Just something different, somewhere else.'

I bought a one-way plane ticket to Coolangatta and on arrival took a bus to Surfers Paradise. A cafe in the main street, hired me even though I had no waitressing experience. At lunchtimes, I sat on the back step with the shrivelled, pale-faced cook and ate roast potatoes that he would bring out hot from the oven until the manager said we couldn't. Every day after work I swam in the surf. One day I got caught in a rip and was swept so far out to sea that the people back on the beach looked like tiny dots. I managed to stop panicking enough for the waves to slowly carry me back to shore and with relief felt firm sand under my feet.

When my roommate in the boarding house where I was living said that she was hitchhiking north, I suggested we hitch together up to my brother Bill's cattle farm, located about five hours' drive north inland. Katie kept going but I stayed with Bill. I cooked and cleaned, and accompanied Bill with his thoroughbred horses to local shows, where we enjoyed socialising with other farmers.

On the farm, after lunch in the hottest part of the day I read from Bill's eclectic collection of books, including James Thurber, Jack Kerouac, John Steinbeck, the Armenian-American William Saroyan and PG Wodehouse. After dinner Bill would select a record from his collection, and the two of us would lie back, legs outstretched, in the big squatters chairs on the wide verandah and listen to jazz musicians—Little Richard, Chuck Berry, Muddy Waters and Eartha Kitt, and the British artists Chris Barber and Ottilie Patterson. Occasionally, Bill's friends would drive over from their farms and we'd all sit around enjoying the music.

* * *

A few years later when you visited the farm as a baby, Robbie, Grandma and Grandpa were always there too, and then Jamie and Megan. You would remember the branches of the huge orange tree that reached over the back steps, with its strong citrus smell and lots of fruit. Were you, like me, wary of the green tree snake which sometimes coiled around its branches?

Down the stairs and over the grass, if we weren't wearing boots, we had to pick our way across the spikey bindii to the back gate leading out to the yards, sheds and paddocks, or to the laundry next to the side fence where the toilet would always be occupied by a couple of startlingly green tree frogs, their skinny legs determinedly grasping at the sides of the bowl, desperate not to be flushed away, again.

I remember you came running to the house one day. You must have been about eight, running to tell Bill, Grandma and me that there was a huge fat python on the laundry floor with bulges along its sides. Remember that? Bill moaned that the python must have swallowed the three white rats he kept in a drum to pregnancy test his thoroughbred mares. You ran back to the laundry and returned to confirm that the drum was indeed empty and that there were exactly three bulges. Bill said the python would sleep until the rats were digested, so you crouched close to study the inert reptile's beautiful, colourful, patterned skin.

As a teenager at the farm, remember how much you loved selecting a book to read from Bill's library? And out in the shed you creatively welded knives from old tins and scraps of metal. We were all very impressed with your skill.

* * *

One morning while I was staying with Bill, early in my year off, I heard the mail van stop. I wandered down through the avenue of kurrajongs to check the roadside letterbox. A litter of lively puppies followed me, jumping and tumbling. After checking there wasn't a snake inside the warm metal drum, I pulled out a bundle of letters.

A blue aerogramme addressed to me in a familiar scrawl stood out. I ripped it open to read while heading back to the house. Sue, my university friend then living in London, had written inviting me to join her on a trip to Ireland. She was leaving in three weeks. I felt a surge of excitement. Of course I'd love to go. What a contrast to life on the farm and a more adventurous way to spend my year of freedom. The letter had taken a week to reach me, so I wondered if I could possibly get back to Melbourne, find my passport, book a flight, get vaccinations, pack a bag, and still make it in time? I decided to go.

Bill was surprised at my sudden departure but organised a lift for me with a friend's mother down to Melbourne. Over the two-day drive south I made a to-do list. Grandma and Grandpa were holidaying in the Flinders Ranges so I couldn't say goodbye to them, but I thought I probably wouldn't be away for long. Plus, I had a plan for when I got back. Bill had agreed that I could lease part of his farm to raise goats. A future of farming appealed to me then, more than teaching.

Back in Melbourne my friend Heather called in. She offered advice on what clothes I should take to the UK, based on her own travelling experiences.

'Take smart clothes for job interviews, restaurants, going to the theatre and concerts,' she said. 'High heels, dresses, jumpers, blouses, stockings.' I packed. My most expensive, most fashionable outfits went into a bulging suitcase which at the airport weighed more than the maximum allowance. Heather kindly helped me unpack and took half the contents home for me.

I left for London, exhausted and excited. The flight attendant passed us our trays of food and I thought about Sue and wondered if she still ate a sticky bun with pink icing as she had in the Monash Uni cafeteria every morning, having always missed breakfast at the university residence where she lived. I wondered if she still played tennis or golf, or if we would play together again, in England. I smiled at remembering how we'd failed our Indonesian poetry essay when we thought we'd written it so cleverly together while drinking her dad's whisky and smoking his cigarettes in the wee hours of the morning at her family farm near Ararat.

I walked dazed for an hour during a fuel stop at Singapore, then slept until touchdown at Heathrow.

Groggily, I staggered through customs and immigration before emerging into daylight and a sea of eager waiting faces. Suddenly I saw Sue at the back of the crowd, waving and grinning. Her curly dark hair was now shoulder length, her face slightly tanned and her tall frame not as thin as the last time I had seen her. I noticed she was wearing faded, torn jeans, an old light-blue polo neck and worn sneakers. Had I brought the wrong clothes?

4

Kindness and Hospitality Everywhere

I would love you to have experienced arriving in London, Robbie. For many expatriates this city represents the centre of the world, being so close to Europe and the United States compared to Australia, South Africa and New Zealand. An advantage for us too is that the language spoken is English, though, with your aptitude for languages, you would have had no difficulty in picking up foreign tongues had you travelled further. I was thrilled to arrive in London to visit a new but surprisingly familiar culture.

'Here, let me take your case,' said Sue, staggering under its weight. 'We'll catch the Tube.'

Thousands of commuters jammed into the train. Before I knew it, we were climbing steep stairs to the street, and then there was Big Ben, straight out of a storybook and backlit by dazzling daylight. Everywhere people were hailing big black square-shaped taxis, and when the taxis stopped, people stepped up, bent over, and walked inside frontwards, rather than sliding in sideways as we did in Melbourne.

'Do you ever catch those, Sue?' I asked.

'No, too expensive,' she said, 'I always walk or catch the Tube.

'Here is where I live, Nevern Mansions, on the third floor.' She led the way up to the front door of a dark red brick, four-storey building.

'People are coming and going from here all the time—Rhodesians, South

Africans, Kiwis, Aussies. We're all expatriates.'

At the top of the stairs we passed several large rooms, including a lounge room with worn upholstered couches. In the kitchen, there were dirty dishes all over the sink.

'Who cleans up?' I asked.

'Anyone who feels like it,' Sue said.

I can picture you, Robbie, enjoying this messy comfortable lifestyle with others your age in London's exciting atmosphere. And your British passport, a valuable asset, would have allowed you to work and live in the United Kingdom indefinitely.

As I stood gazing around, Sue dived into the fridge and emerged sniffing a bottle of milk.

'It's still okay,' she said happily. 'Here, have some cornflakes.'

It was early afternoon, but to Sue, cornflakes were right for any meal. 'We'll dump your stuff in the bedroom then go out to meet some of the others.'

That was when I first set eyes on your dad, Robbie. He was one of Sue's friends, lined up waiting for tickets outside the Royal Albert Hall.

Sue introduced me to Bertie, Garth and Ben. Garth wasn't tall but I thought he was handsome. He was dressed casually and neatly, in tan corduroy trousers and a fine wool green jumper over a collared shirt.

While Sue talked to Bert and Ben, Garth and I stood apart and chatted comfortably. He had what I thought was a cultured accent and asked me about our plans, then listened with interest to my answer. I felt a surge of excitement during this conversation and went away thinking about how charming he was.

I was impressed by his politeness and by his hair, which stuck out afro-style, all tight dark brown curls. I asked Sue when we might see her friends again. She said we'd be seeing them all the next night for a game of tennis.

But then Garth sent a message to say that he couldn't make it to tennis because he had to work that night, cleaning a hospital. I was told later that he was working two jobs for extra money to travel.

'How disappointing,' I said. His interesting voice had kept coming into my thoughts and I'd wondered what he'd be like at tennis.

'We'll be with them again in Kent when we get back from Ireland,' said Sue. 'We're all going hop-picking.'

That night Sue and I went to watch a free outdoor performance of *A Midsummer Night's Dream* in St James's Park. It felt surreal. It was as if I was living inside one of my childhood storybooks. I wondered if tomorrow when we went to see the Changing of the Guard, would Christopher Robin be at the gates of Buckingham Palace?

You had a much broader range of children's books to read than the limited range I had during the 1950s, Robbie. You devoured books by Roald Dahl, Madeleine L'Engle, CS Lewis, JRR Tolkien, O.Henry, EB White and numerous other authors.

When Sue and I returned to Earl's Court that night, we discussed the clothes that we'd need for our trip.

'We won't be doing any job interviews, at least none that require such smart clothes,' Sue laughed.

All we needed, she said, would be jeans, two shirts, a pair of sneakers, an anorak. I had none of those. Sue said I had to swap my suitcase for a backpack too.

You, Robbie, always wore flannies with shorts or jeans and sneakers, so would have had the ideal clothes for this trip.

* * *

Sue's friend Faye, a bright, bubbly and friendly Londoner, drove us expertly through the heavy London traffic and then out of the city and across to Wales to the port of Fishguard.

On the drive I quizzed Sue about her friends who I'd met on my first day in London. She said that Garth had a van that cost fifty pounds and was pushed by its passengers more often than it was driven. Apparently lots of expatriates bought old vehicles to travel in and then sold them cheaply when they settled down or returned to their home country.

In Ireland the grass was not only green but thick and soft, so unlike most camping spots I'd seen in Australia.

How much you loved camping. Your dad did too, especially when we lived in the Hunter Valley. One of our favourite camping spots was behind the beach in the trees at Seal Rocks, on the New South Wales coast. Remember how when the sand was so hot around the tent we'd all run on our heels, squealing down to the water? After years of not wearing shoes, your feet had become more like hard leather than skin. You often carried Megan across the scorching sand. At night we'd smother ourselves with Rid to ward off the mosquitoes and ticks. In the daytime we looked out for snakes, and in the late afternoon we'd all sit on the cooling sand and watch the sea and sky change colour while munching on chips. You children would drink lemonade while your dad and I would have a "snort" of beer.

Camping in Ireland on that lush green grass was not better, but easier. Neither Faye nor Sue had an itinerary and I was just along for fun, so we were in no hurry. Faye drove—at Sue's and my urging—along back roads, frequently pulling up at picturesque village pubs. There would be a cosy, lounge-like main room with a fire blazing and men playing darts or dominoes. We drank Guinness and listened fascinated as they told us stories about the poverty in the countryside and the Troubles up north.

I think that you, Robbie, would have enjoyed camping on soft Irish grass and drinking in the friendly pubs. The locals would tell you tales in their lilting accents and in return enjoy your Australian stories.

One night Sue, Faye and I were sitting around the campfire when a dishevelled young man ran out of the dark and approached us. He was distraught. In a heavy accent he told us how a girl in his group of German hikers had fallen and broken her leg. She was a medical student who was being brave but was in great pain. We immediately all leapt into our car and drove him to the nearest town in the Ring of Kerry for help. He stayed with the police as they called on others to mount a rescue. A couple of hours later, back at our camp, we watched torch lights zigzagging slowly down the mountain through thick fog, accompanied by sweet loud singing.

After two weeks Faye had to get back to work in London. We said goodbye at the ferry. At a quaint tobacconist Sue and I bought a tin of Holbrook tobacco each and a packet of cigarette papers, cheaper than factory-made cigarettes we reasoned, and sat on a bench to practise rolling one. We then set out to hitchhike north.

I'm telling you about my trip with Sue in Ireland, Robbie, because I can picture you enjoying that beautiful country as much as we did. Perhaps you would have hiked or rock climbed in the Ring of Kerry, or swum through underwater caves. You might have jumped off high platforms and leapt into the clear blue Atlantic Ocean, not far from Killarney.

Sue and I never had to wait long for a lift. The driver would ask us about Australia and whether we knew his cousin or his brother or his neighbour who might have moved to Perth or Melbourne or Sydney. Some of them looked surprised, and some disappointed when we said we didn't. That first day we made it over the border of Northern Ireland.

'Enniskillen hasn't been affected by the Troubles, so you'll be safe,' our driver, a gently spoken man in his fifties, told us as we got out. We decided it was too late to find a field, plus it was starting to rain, so we clambered into the back of an empty truck parked in a depot and snuggled into our sleeping bags. We were both sound asleep when we heard an explosion, or was it a shooting? We sat bolt upright in the dark, listening for more sounds, whispering to each other. How close was it? It sounded close. Could this government truck yard be a target? Might we be discovered, or worse, shot at? Or might the trucks be set on fire? Should we stay or should we get out of here? Where could we go in the middle of the night?

Then through the crackling static of Sue's little transistor radio we heard that for the first time violence had broken out in Enniskillen. We took out our recently purchased tins of tobacco and each rolled a cigarette. As quietness returned, we fell asleep again.

The next morning we tentatively picked our way through the glass shards in the street. We nodded a greeting to the stony-faced shopkeeper who was out with a broom sweeping up. The explosive noises had not been gunfire or bombs, but rocks thrown through shop windows.

'Adults teach children to hate the other side,' our next driver told us. 'Gang violence is becoming the norm here.' At Newry, he said, 'I'll drop you at a hotel.'

'Thanks but we'll find a field to sleep in,' Sue said.

'There's a youth hostel here, how about I drop you there?'

'No, thanks, we'll be okay.'

The driver spoke to a policeman on traffic duty about us.

'It's too dangerous to sleep in a field,' the officer said. 'You can sleep in the station but wait until after the pubs close, in case I need the cell after an arrest.'

We hung around in the pub wishing we were curled up in our sleeping bags but pleased at the thought of sleeping in a police cell. We didn't know anyone who had slept in a police cell before. But when we got to the station, we found that a local drunk was already in our 'room'.

'Well,' the officer said, 'it's too late to find somewhere else tonight, so if you're gone in the morning before the supervisor arrives, you can sleep in the waiting room. It's quite cosy.'

'No worries,' we said, as we climbed into our sleeping bags.

In the morning, we awoke to see a tall, uniformed police officer standing at the door, smiling and holding a tray with a teapot, a jug of milk, a bowl of sugar, three cups and a saucer of sweet biscuits. As we drank our tea he plied us with questions about where we were from, why we were travelling, the adventures we'd had so far and where we were going next. The supervisor was a practised interrogator, and he was genuinely interested in our answers. He told us he'd like to go to Australia one day.

Years later, sitting at home in Wahroonga with you, I heard on the morning news that a policeman had been killed in a bomb blast in the Newry Police Station. I told you about the kindness those policemen had shown to Sue and me and how sad I was that the Troubles' violence continued to bring tragedy to families.

Sue and I spent the next night sleeping on straw, sheltered from the rain in a barn in County Antrim. The day after, we began working for a local family, the Smiths, helping harvest their potatoes. The locals were wide-eyed when Sue and I took out our tins of tobacco and rolled our cigarettes at smoko. Twice a day we ate potatoes, fresh and delicious.

Once their crop was harvested, the Smiths arranged for us to contract pick. We hopped onto the back of a truck that took us to a field near Belfast, from where we could hear explosions. Here the potatoes were small and the ground was muddy. In one morning Sue and I together only managed to fill half a box.

We collected our pay, about a pound between us, and hopped on a bus to Belfast.

Thick boards covered shopfronts. The atmosphere was strained, eerie. Few citizens but many soldiers were in the streets. One soldier told us to stand facing a wall with our hands up and frisked first Sue then me. It wasn't a city to hang about in, so we bought a bottle of beer and took it to the Smiths'. We offered to babysit the children for a night. It was the least we could do in return for their weeks of generosity and kindness. The next day the whole Smith family came as they drove us to Larne to catch the ferry to England. We all cried and hugged our goodbyes.

'We'll write and will come back one day,' we said.

We wrote once, but never visited them again.

5

Adapting to Changes

It's funny, Robbie, how we can plot and plan our future, both short and long term, and how often something totally different happens. Sue and I were soon to discover that we relished unexpected opportunities.

At the Larne ferry terminal, Keith, an English truck driver, offered us a lift. We explained that we were heading to join friends who were hop-picking in Kent. Amazingly, Keith's destination was Kent.

Sue said that Garth, Bertie and Ben would be surprised to see us so soon. I was excited at the thought of seeing Sue's friends again within a day or so and wondered if we would work together on the hop farm. We climbed up into Keith's cabin.

'Lie down so nobody can see you,' he said. 'That way you won't have to pay.' We slunk down out of sight. Keith drove slowly down under the deck of the ferry into the area where vehicles parked during the crossing.

'You can sit up now,' he said.

We stared through his windscreen at two huge double tankers in front of us, both leaking water.

'What's in those massive tankers?' I asked.

'Eels going to Holland.'

I glanced at Sue. She understood.

'Would you mind, Keith, if we ask them for a lift instead?'

Surprised, Keith watched as we climbed down out of his cabin and approached the two Dutch drivers. Next thing, we were running back to him.

'Thanks, Keith, but we're going to Holland now.'

'What about hop-picking in Kent and meeting up with your friends?'

'That will have to wait.'

Although I had looked forward to meeting up with the boys I'd met in London, the chance to go to Europe in an eel truck was too exciting to pass up.

* * *

Robbie, remember when we set off for Bill's farm with a definite plan in mind that was changed on the way?

Grandma and Grandpa had driven Jamie and Megan to Queensland for the school holidays, but you were performing a piano recital in Wahroonga, so you and I were driving up together a few days later.

We set off on time. We had been happily chatting for about three hours and were following a truck when a rock flew like a missile into the windscreen, shattering it into millions of shards. I stopped to knock a hole in it with a shoe so I could see the road. Our map showed that the nearest town was behind us, about half an hour back.

It was midafternoon by the time the windscreen was replaced and we set off again. Because we had lost so many hours, I kept driving well after dark, expecting to stay in a motel though we hadn't booked anywhere. When I felt too tired to drive further we decided to stay the night in the next town.

The first motel had a NO VACANCY sign displayed. The second motel did also. The third motel's manager shook his head and said that not only was he booked out, so was every one of the ten motels in town because there was a bowling convention on. Desperate, I pleaded if he could suggest anywhere that might have a room. After thinking hard, he said there was an old pub a few miles out of town that might.

We detoured. Yes, the female licensee had one room and it had two single beds. We could tie the dog up to our car out the back. The kitchen was closed, but the cook prepared us a steak, which was welcome. You were asleep the minute your head hit the pillow.

I must have gone to sleep because I was awakened by scuffles and yelling on the upstairs verandah outside our flimsy French doors. It sounded violent and close and I was scared that bodies would crash through into our room. I thought you'd be worried, but I was stiff with fear and didn't want to make a sound. Then a high-pitched female voice screamed out from below and I heard the men instantly racing off and shimmying down the verandah posts. All was quiet. You hadn't stirred.

We left early the next morning with frost thick on the ground. Half an hour later a huge kangaroo came out of nowhere and crashed into the driver's door. It rolled over the bonnet and limped off into the bush. A strip of metal had fallen off the car, but initially I didn't think it was important. Then I changed my mind, let Buster out for a run and you and I walked back to pick the piece of metal up. It only took a couple of minutes, but that was long enough for Buster to roll around in a dead carcass and for the smell to make me gag. For fresh air I opened the car windows, but you found the cold worse than the stench. We weren't in such a happy frame of mind now. But it's fun looking back on that adventure, when our plans were not exactly derailed, but certainly made more colourful.

* * *

Now in Europe, Sue and I found ourselves sitting in a cafe by a canal in Amsterdam, drinking coffee and rolling cigarettes. Alcohol was freely available too—cafes sold beer and wine, in stark contrast to cafes in Australia, but I didn't see anyone intoxicated.

At the Rijksmuseum we gazed in awe at the Old Dutch Masters. The figures in the portraits expressed dignity, like the people out on the streets of Amsterdam.

About two years later when I studied the masterpieces at the Louvre Museum in Paris, I was cradling you in my arms. You were an artist from a young age, so I'd love to know which of these magnificent pieces you'd choose as your favourites. Amazingly, in paintings of large groups, every face depicted was a portrait.

Sue and I decided to hitchhike to the home of my old school friend, Valerie, who lived further south across the border at Waterloo, in Belgium. This is when Sue and I had an unplanned and undesirable adventure.

* * *

At a table in a service station cafe, Sue told me about the need for rules when hitchhiking in Europe. 'Having some rules and sticking to them makes hitching safer.'

A man wearing a red cap at the next table asked us where we were heading.

'Waterloo,' we said.

He looked at his companion. They nodded at each other. 'We're going there,' his companion said in a strong French accent. 'We can take you.'

We followed them out to their car, a late-model red Renault. Strong Accent opened the boot and told us to put in our backpacks.

'No,' said Sue firmly. 'We'll keep them with us.'

The men looked annoyed. Why should it matter to them if our packs were in the boot or the back with us? I wondered. I also wondered why Sue was so insistent.

'You,' said Strong Accent, indicating to me, 'sit in the front, and you,' he looked at Sue, 'sit in the back.'

'No,' said Sue, 'we'll sit together in the back.'

Again, her insistence puzzled me. Then I remembered, Sue had rules. These must be two of them. I was happy to go along with her decisions. We'd been driving for well over two hours, and it was starting to get dark. There were no buildings in sight, let alone a town.

'Where are we?' Sue asked in English.

'Going to Waterloo,' answered Red Cap, who was driving.

'We should have arrived,' Sue said. 'We've been driving for two and a half hours.' Now she was listening to the men's conversation as we drove along an isolated dirt road. Sue had already spent some time travelling in France, so was confident in speaking the language. She listened intently as Red Cap and Strong Accent spoke to each other. The expression on her face frightened me as she muttered in my ear, 'The car will slow down soon. As soon as it stops, grab your pack and run.'

I tensed and pulled my pack close. The car did slow. As we negotiated a hairpin bend, I grabbed the door handle. I opened the door just before we stopped then I was out and off, powered by adrenaline, sprinting down the road. I heard yelling behind me. Where was Sue? Why wasn't she running too? I heard her shouting and turned around to see her struggling with Strong Accent. Red Cap was walking around the car to join in.

What should I do? Keep going to get help? If I go back, they'll have us both. Risk that? On one side of the road was a pine forest and on the other a field. There was not a light or a house in sight. I turned back to fight. I'd only gone a few metres when, with an alarming scream and a hefty push of her backpack into Strong Accent's chest, Sue broke away and ran flat out towards me. We crashed through the field's fence and rolled down a slope.

Back in their Renault with its lights on high beam, the men cruised slowly backwards and forwards along the stretch of road where they had last seen us. From the ditch, we could hear them talking in low voices through the car's open windows. The lights shone into the forest and onto the fields, but we kept our heads down.

We had been crouching uncomfortably for what felt like ages when they gave up and drove off. Tired and cold and with no idea of our whereabouts, we decided to sleep where we were. We climbed into our sleeping bags. It was a while before we calmed down enough to sleep. Sue blamed herself for accepting the ride.

'But you followed your rules,' I said. 'Without them it could have been much worse.'

From then on, we decided that we would only accept a lift from a single person or a family.

In the morning we realised we had slept in a cow field. We climbed through the fence we'd plunged through the night before, which now felt mildly electric, and walked a kilometre or more along a dirt track until we reached a bitumen road.

Hitchhikers rarely faced danger and in the seventies it was a favourite means of transport, especially popular in the UK and Europe. In Australia hitchhiking became less and less accepted as a means of travel. Attacks, even murders, occurred and were well-publicised. I never suggested that you hitchhike, and to my knowledge you never did nor did any of your friends.

It was afternoon by the time Sue and I arrived at Valerie and Ewan's. Ewan had kindly picked us up from the bus stop and said that he hoped our visit would cheer Valerie up as she was unhappy. I explained to them both what had happened to us over the past twenty-four hours. Knowing me from when we were both students at a private all-girls school in Melbourne, Valerie was unimpressed.

'Why would you choose to put yourselves in such danger?' she asked.

I told her that hitchhiking was fun, that we had met some fascinating people, and that yesterday was the first bad experience we had had.

'I'm sorry I wasn't of more comfort to Valerie,' I said to Ewan in the car on the way to the bus stop the next day.

'That's okay, you're on an adventure,' he replied, leaving us to wait for a bus heading further south over the border into France.

A green Mercedes soon stopped, driven by a ruggedly handsome, middle-aged Englishman. 'Where are you headed?' he asked.

'Anywhere in France,' Sue replied.

The Englishman's name was Chris Newman, and he had designed a mature-tree digger, which he was displaying to sell to civic landscapers to use to plant large trees.

In return for stories of our life in Australia, which he said broke the boredom for him, we travelled with him, staying in French inns and eating at restaurants. I ate snails cooked in butter and garlic, for the first time. They were chewy, but delicious.

During these lazy days in France, Sue, Chris and I shared picnics of baguettes, salami and cheese. I lay on the grass in the sun looking up at the blue French sky. I smiled, only faintly aware of Sue and Chris murmuring in the background. I enjoyed that no-one apart from them knew where in the world I was. In my mind I was floating like an object out at sea, subject to the whims of the wind and the tide.

6

A Friendship Develops

Having arrived back in London, Chris asked where we were going next.

'Scotland,' said Sue.

We had planned to hitchhike and meet up with Bert, Ben and Garth, who were travelling together from London in a van. I was excited. This trip promised to be fun as I pictured the neatly dressed, handsome Garth of medium height and brown curly hair who had sparked my interest after only one encounter.

On hearing Sue's answer, Chris offered to lend us his wife's car, a station wagon. Tricia was away with Claire visiting relatives in New Zealand. We were delighted with this offer. Not only did we have free transport but also free and comfortable accommodation because we could sleep in the back. Chris picked us up from the Tring station, then waved us off with the car and a bottle of Scottish whisky.

We bought a packet of cornflakes and a bottle of milk and set off in convoy with Ben, Bert and Garth, who were travelling together in a van. After first meeting these three boys briefly six weeks ago, I liked the prospect of travelling with and getting to know them.

By dusk on the first night, we had made it to the Lake District and the Drunken Duck Inn. On the walls were posters of Guinness and paintings of hunters in red riding coats, sitting tall on sleek horses surrounded by packs of eager beagles. The dark timber floorboards creaked as we walked in. Garth and I ended up sitting next to each other in old leather armchairs in front of a crackling fire.

'Have you tried a chaser?' he asked.

'A what?' I replied.

'You drink a dram of whisky, then follow it with a beer.'

I quickly discovered that one chaser was more than enough for me and happily listened as Garth talked, with my prompting, about what it had been like to grow up in South Africa. From that conversation on, Robbie, I started to learn about your dad's childhood.

He said that he had gone to a boarding school in Natal that had enforced strong discipline based on the model of elite English boarding schools. This education explained his lovely accent and manners, I thought. He only saw his parents a few times a year when, like most of the boys, he caught the train home to Johannesburg. Your dad told me about his holidays as a boy camping and going to game reserves with his father, Rex.

One of his father's friends, George, had a private reserve. A warden protected the game from poachers and your dad had slept in the open with wild game nearby and only one man on duty, awake, to keep them safe. I thought how brave they all were and I could see how much your dad loved the bush and its wildlife.

'What about your life in Australia?' he asked, so I told him about an incident that had happened on Bill's farm just before I had left for England.

'I had driven up the back paddock in the ute to check the troughs for water and to make sure the windmill was working,' I began. 'But I drove the ute over an anthill and got it stuck. I tried to dig it out with a rifle I found in the back. Semis roaring past along the highway to Rockie were unlikely to stop for me, so I walked back to the house to ask Bill for help. I found him welding a gate in the shed. It had taken about half an hour to trudge back over rough ground and I was sweating from the heat. Bill turned off the welder, took off his mask, grabbed a shovel and walked back to the anthill to dig the ute out.'

Your dad looked puzzled.

'What?' I asked.

'What's a ute, a semi and Rockie?' Being from South Africa, he knew about anthills.

As the whisky and beer chasers continued, the three boys ribbed each other continuously, making us laugh. Your dad used to always make me laugh.

Having no set plan, we drove wherever the road took us, spending hours in pubs when it rained, which was frequently.

One day, we took a ferry across to the Isle of Skye where we hunted around on the windy golf links for equipment until, in a dilapidated old clubhouse, we found a few balls, an iron and a wood. Sue, Bert and I hit our first balls off course, but your dad teed off with a drive that flew far and straight down the middle of the fairway. I was impressed by his relaxed golf swing and how far and accurately he could hit a golf ball. I hoped there would be more chances to play with him.

Back on the mainland, through stunning mountainous scenery, we drove towards Fort William and camped there overnight.

'Should I climb Ben Nevis?' I asked Garth the next morning.

'Of course, why not?' he asked.

'My socks and shoes are saturated from walking in the rain yesterday. I'll have to wear thongs.'

'That would be unusual footwear for a mountain climb,' he said. 'But it's up to you. You can always turn back if it's too hard.'

So, we all set off up the highest mountain in Britain on an ice-covered track. I was soon aware of small pebbles and sharp stones pushing into the skin under my feet. They didn't hurt too much, so I kept going. Near the top, after climbing for more than two hours, Sue and I decided not to do the last stretch to the summit, but the three boys continued. When they came down we were sitting near the van, drinking tea and rolling cigarettes. The boys excitedly told us about how they had been caught in a snowstorm and couldn't see a thing, let alone the legendary view.

Then Garth looked at my feet. They had turned a bluish colour. 'How do they feel?' he asked.

'I can't feel them at all,' I said. 'I think stones are stuck under the soles of my feet.'

'I'll have a look,' he said. Sitting cross-legged on the ground near me, your dad cradled my left foot in his warm hands, studied the sole and frowned. 'There are stones here. I'll dig them out. Where's your pocketknife?'

I fossicked around in the outer pocket of my backpack and handed it to him. 'It's probably a bit dirty,' I said.

Your dad flicked it open, ran his finger along the sharp edge of the blade and wiped it across his jumper. In one hand he held my foot tenderly, picking out stones with the other. I expected a lot of blood, but he was careful not to gouge deep, and I suppose my foot was too cold to bleed much.

'Some are tiny, like gravel,' he said. 'Does it hurt?' he asked, and determinedly dug at a deeper one.

I couldn't feel anything. My feet were numb.

'Now the other one,' he said. 'This foot has more.' He finished and flicked my little pile of stones at Bert, who batted them away with a stick. Garth took both of my feet between his hands until the feeling in them returned. As the warmth brought back feeling, pain surged too. He fished around in his backpack and pulled out a pair of clean, thick, khaki woollen socks. 'Here, put these on,' he said. That night, he and I slept in the station wagon while Sue slept in the van with the others.

From Fort William, we headed north to camp by the famous Loch Ness.

'Coming for a swim anyone?' I asked. Only I went in.

'Watch out for the monster,' yelled Ben.

I laughed, but instinctively scanned the surface for any sign of rippling. The lake water was freezing, but I badly needed a wash, and this was a rare opportunity.

So, Robbie, your dad and I were becoming intimate as we travelled together during carefree days, far from South Africa and Australia. I admired his ease at finding suitable camping spots and in setting up a campsite. He did much of the driving over those weeks and with him I felt safe and happy.

I loved Scotland and the Scots, even though we often struggled to understand what they were saying. The scenery was stunning, but I was more impressed by who was in the car than what was outside. As we headed south again to London, I came to realise that I didn't care where we were really, as long as I was with your dad. I loved snuggling up to him at night, cosy in the back of the station wagon. If only we could keep going inseparably, indefinitely.

* * *

Back in London, your dad and I headed to his rental flat in Holland Park. He offered to make a late lunch. 'Mashed potato sandwich, okay?' he asked, looking into a near-empty fridge. Then, out of the blue, he suggested that we go to see *Swan Lake* at Covent Garden. I had told him how much I had enjoyed going to see the ballet in Melbourne.

'I'd love to but isn't it expensive?' I asked.

'Not if we go up in the gods. Let's see if we can get tickets for tonight.'

We raced out to catch the tube to Covent Garden, ran to the ticket box and bought the cheap tickets, then leapt up the stairs, then more stairs, then more.

Breathless by the time we reached the top, and standing, as there were no seats up there, I peered down at the rest of the audience below. They looked so small. I wondered if it would be worth it.

Then the orchestra started playing Tchaikovsky's sad, haunting opening theme and I became mesmerised by the slim female dancers, clad in wispy white, as they glided and pirouetted. In contrast, the male dancers in tights caught them with powerful strength, then gracefully leapt across the stage.

'Wasn't that wonderful?' I said to Garth on our way home to his flat.

'Yes,' he said. He put his arm around me and kissed my cheek.

The next morning we hitchhiked to Cornwall, where we searched for a bothy. 'What about that?' Garth said, pointing to a horse float in an isolated field.

'But what about the slope?' I said.

'As long as our heads are at the up end, we'll be fine,' he said. He swept out the dried horse pats with a broom and unrolled our sleeping bags. The float was now invitingly cosy. That night we snuggled up, unaffected by the angle.

The next day we hitchhiked to Land's End, the most westerly point of England, with our meagre supplies of a few raw potatoes, a small gas ring, and a pot. We were looking forward to eating boiled potatoes high on a cliff looking out to the Celtic Sea and the English Channel, but when we got there the wind was icy and blowing so hard that I struggled, first to light the gas cooker, and then to keep the flame going.

We stood with our backs to the coast to buffer the wind. The water boiled for a few minutes before the flame went out. I struck match after match but, in the end, we nibbled uncooked potatoes that were only just warm.

'When we get to a village, I'm buying Cornish pasties, I love them,' I said.

Your Grandma's grandfather, Robbie, was a Cornish tin miner before he sailed to Tasmania and opened a gold mine. She told me how the miners would take a pasty for lunch that was meat and vegetables at one end and apple at the other end, a neat two-course meal. The next day your dad and I hitchhiked to the nearby village and feasted on a meat and potato Cornish pasty each. Yum.

We found a centuries-old church with elaborate brass plaques featuring knights in full armour on its floor and walls. Before leaving London, we had gone to an art shop and selected papers and crayon-type chalk. 'Black crayon on white paper or gold crayon on black paper is effective,' your dad had said.

Now, he crouched down and spread a length of white paper over an imposing armoured figure and started rubbing over it with a black crayon. He was very precise and it showed his eye for detail. Kneeling, I placed a piece of black paper over a scene depicting women and children in smocks and started rubbing with a gold crayon. When we held the rubbings up to show each other, we were both pleased with the results. We carefully rolled them so they wouldn't crease and put them in a cardboard roll your dad had for carrying them. I dropped a few coins in a box at the front of the church as thanks.

Robbie, you have seen a few of these rubbings hanging on the walls in our house, sombre in their black frames.

*   *   *

The first cracks in this idyllic lifestyle appeared when, on the road, waiting for the next lift, I was startled to hear your dad say, a little hesitantly, that when we got back to London he would have to meet up with Roslyn to organise their trip.

I felt a surge of panic. The timeless bubble I'd floated in with your dad was about to burst. Surely he wouldn't still follow through on the plan he'd made with Roslyn, whom he'd met hop-picking months ago?

On our first day of travelling to Scotland together, Garth had told me that Roslyn, a New Zealander, had asked him to accompany her backpacking across Afghanistan, Pakistan and India on her way back home. Garth had wanted to end up in Australia, so he had agreed. I suppose I had just hoped it wouldn't happen. The purpose of the meeting at Roslyn's sister's flat in Hammersmith was to discuss details. I didn't want to meet Roslyn and her sister, but Garth said it would be good if I went, so I did.

Roslyn, a redhead, gave me a cool reception and ignored me for the rest of the evening, but I could sense there was no romantic connection with Garth, which was some relief. Her older sister, Leah, told me that Roslyn had been counting on Garth to travel with her because the trip would be far too dangerous for a girl on her own. Roslyn had been looking forward to it for months and would be heartbroken if Garth pulled out now. I just wished she could have found someone else.

Roslyn had already spread out the dried food she and Garth would need for the trip. On the kitchen bench were bowls of oats, dates, raisins, dried apricots, dried apples, almonds, cinnamon and dried milk powder. We chopped the fruit and nuts into small pieces. We put a mixture of the ingredients into small plastic bags and sealed them tight. Each pack now contained a nutritious meal that just needed the addition of water. She and Garth set a date for their departure.

On our way back to Garth's flat, he and I were quiet.

'What will you do now?' he asked me.

'I'm not sure,' I said. 'I could visit Cyprus and stay with my cousin George's relatives, and maybe get a job there. Or I could visit some Middle Eastern countries and maybe go to Israel to work on a kibbutz.'

Your dad said he would have liked to go with me to these places. So, we discussed a compromise. We would travel together by bus to Italy and then by boat to Egypt. He and I would visit Lebanon, then he would leave me to fly to Rome to meet Roslyn and accompany her overland, out of Europe and across Asia to New Zealand and Australia. He and I would eventually meet up again in Australia.

'We'll need some more bags of muesli,' I said. So, we bought more ingredients for me and packaged them up, ready for a long bus ride.

I asked Sue what she thought about Garth sticking to his former plan to travel with Roslyn even though he and I had become so close.

'I know you'll miss him,' she said. 'But it's not for long.'

Sue told me that she had hoped I would continue travelling with her after Garth had left. So, Robbie, me choosing Garth over Sue to travel with at that point was a pivotal moment, because it led to dramatic and unforeseen circumstances.

I was grateful to Sue, who had taught me how to travel on a shoestring. "The less we spend, the further we can go," was her mantra. I asked her once what she remembered most about our time travelling together, thinking she would pick a country or particular experience, but she said it was laughing.

I was leaving London for another adventure with your dad, who was quiet, witty and made me laugh. I wrote an aerogramme to your Grandma and Grandpa telling them of my latest plans, but with only a vague outline of the countries I might visit. I didn't want to worry them. When I'd written to them before, I hadn't mentioned hitchhiking or sleeping in fields, or much about my travelling companions, apart from Sue, who they knew.

On your dad's arrival from Johannesburg, he had worked in and around London for John Stewart's English civil engineering firm, and had cycled to the office near Marble Arch. John Stewart was an old friend of Rex, your other Grandfather. John was Garth's godfather, who—along with his wife, Helen, and their two children, Jean and John junior—had left the apartheid regime in South Africa to settle permanently in England. Helen invited your dad and me to lunch at their elegant house in Cobham, Surrey, on our last Sunday in England. They wished us well for our journey.

'Keep in touch,' Helen said as we kissed goodbye.

None of us then had any idea of the importance we would later play in each other's lives.

7

Together in The Middle East

Your dad and I were now on our way to the Middle East. At each stop on our bus trip across Europe, we would tear open the seal on our plastic bags of oats and fruit. The stops would be just long enough for us to boil some water on our portable gas ring and stir it into our bowls of muesli. We would eat hungrily, stomping our feet to keep warm. It was November, the start of winter.

Your dad told me how when he was at boarding school, as a punishment, he had had to run around the frosty oval in bare feet.

'After ten minutes, I had no feeling below my knees,' he said.

'What had you done for such a punishment? I asked.

'Nothing much. A lot of punishment was meted out by the senior boys, not the masters.'

'What did your mum and Rex say about that?'

'Dad had fought in the war. He agreed with strong discipline.'

Now, I see why your dad could sympathise with me when my feet were frozen after climbing Ben Nevis in thongs.

When our bus arrived at the Italian port of Brindisi on the Mediterranean, we boarded a boat that took us to the top of the African continent and the Egyptian port of Alexandria. We caught a bus to Egypt's capital, Cairo, on the Nile River.

Cairo was a smelly, noisy, colourful city, full of men hurrying by in kaftans and women in black abayas and hijabs. A few of the women wore *boshiyas*, the Arab version of the burqa, so that no part of their bodies were visible except for their eyes. Even in winter Cairo was hot, and I wondered how they coped with the heat.

A boy waved and called us over to what he called his cafe. We sat at a small worn wooden table and ordered apple tea. The boy called another boy and gave him our order. The second boy hurried off.

We watched as similar boys weaved their way through the crowded streets all around us, holding trays of bread and small glasses of what looked like black coffee high above their heads, almost invisible apart from the one hand that balanced the tray.

Our order appeared, held high above the second boy's head. He lowered the tea to our table.

As we sipped our tea, piping hot and sweet, from little coloured glasses, your dad told me how Rex had visited Cairo during the war.

I mentioned this to your brother recently, who told me more about Rex's stay in Egypt. Jamie has an interest in wartime accounts, and told me that after Rex had died, Garth and his younger brother, your Uncle Danny, offered Rex's war medals to him. Rex had served in the South African Engineer Corps under British Command and was one of the Allied soldiers fighting in North Africa against German General Rommel's famous Afrika Korps and its Panzer tanks. With the medals was a handwritten diary of his wartime in North Africa.

Rex wrote that they fought battles across vast stretches of flat desert. The few elevated positions in the landscape were hard-fought because they gave some perspective on the enemy positions. One day Rex ran, on his own and under heavy fire, to the German trenches. Once he reached them he shot all the occupants and claimed the trench for the Allies. After the war was over, King George VI presented him with a Member of Order of the British Empire Medal at a ceremony in London. He also was awarded a Military Cross and Distinguished Service Order.

When Jamie told me this, Robbie, I realised that you weren't the only risk-taker in the family.

Cairo was crowded. Garth and I pushed through the throngs of people at the fruit and vegetable markets with their stalls full of vibrant reds, yellows, greens and purples—melons, grapes, beans, tomatoes and capsicums stacked high on barrows. A bagful of each only cost a few piastres, the equivalent of an Australian dollar at the time. We found a cheap youth hostel and made a delicious meal in the communal kitchen.

The next day we walked past a street seller's display of flavoured milk, the coloured bottles lined up neatly on a shelf, and your dad looked at them thirstily.

'Are they sealed?' I asked, doubting they could be. 'Is that milk fresh? Pasteurised?' The vendor nodded. Had he understood?

'I'll have to drink one,' your dad said, gazing at them longingly. 'I haven't had a drink of milk for ages.' Garth pointed and looked at the street vendor. 'A white one.' He handed the vendor a few piastres and gulped the milk down.

Less than an hour later, we found ourselves rushing to find the nearest public toilet where your dad heaved out milk and more. We didn't go too far from a toilet for the rest of that day. I spent much of it standing outside, gazing at the locals going about their everyday activities. While many women wore black, the children, both boys and girls, wore ordinary Western-style clothes—coloured shorts, T-shirts and jumpers. They seemed happy, and many approached me, albeit shyly, wanting, it seemed, to try out their few words of English. Gesticulating and laughing, the children and I communicated a little, but I couldn't explain what I was doing loitering near a public toilet.

Outside the Museum of Cairo, massive stone statues of sphinxes, too heavy for thieves to easily remove, gave us a taste of what lay inside. As well as giant statues of pharaohs, there was exquisite jewellery in glass cases, highly decorated knives and fragments of walls featuring mysterious hieroglyphics.

We didn't notice any security guards, and we could walk right up to the sarcophagus of the boy king Tutankhamun to admire his gold funeral mask. I remember marvelling at how the artist had depicted his face and especially his open staring eyes.

At Giza, your dad and I slipped away from the crowds and climbed up the Great Pyramid by ourselves. I read at the museum that it was made four and a half thousand years ago, using two million perfectly chiselled solid sandstone blocks which covered mysterious tunnels and chambers where the pharaoh King Khufu was laid with the treasure he might need for the next life.

Guides hawking tours yelled at us as your dad and I continued climbing. At the time, your dad didn't talk about the Great Pyramid as a marvel of human engineering but, I think being an engineer, he must have found it fascinating. I know you would have enjoyed climbing it and investigating its origins.

Further south, in Luxor, in the Valley of the Kings, we walked down tunnels where other pharaohs had been entombed after their death. We played hide-and-seek around the massive columns of Thebes.

We caught a train and travelled in the third-class carriage to Aswan, where we stayed in the youth hostel, which typically had segregated dormitories.

During the night I awoke, aware of someone in the room. A large figure was sitting on the end of my bed. I told him to turn on the light, which revealed a handsome fair-haired man with startling green eyes who spoke softly, telling me not to be frightened.

I asked why he was in my room. The manager of the hostel had told him, he said, that I was an Australian and possibly leaving the next day. He had to see me tonight as he wanted my help to get to Australia.

'Why?' I asked.

The man told me that his name was Abdul-Rabhe, that he was an Afghani who had got a teaching job in Saudi Arabia, because it was hard to get a teaching job in Afghanistan, but he had been forced to witness a woman being stoned in the village square. He had found that horrible and was desperate to move to a good country, like Australia.

I would have liked to have helped him, but how could I?

The next morning your dad was indignant when I told him about my night visitor and wanted to confront him, but I told him what a sad situation Abdul-

Rab was in. The Afghani had thought I, a stranger who was fortunate enough to be born in a country where teaching jobs are plentiful and women are not publicly stoned to death, could help him realise a dream.

8

Romantic Beirut

After Egypt your dad and I were excited to be heading to Lebanon. At the ferry terminal in Alexandria we found hundreds of people milling and jostling around the wharf, and only one boat. There didn't seem to be any officials in charge, so tickets were irrelevant and brute force was the only thing needed to board.

Desperate passengers aggressively pushed through each other to access the gangway, ignoring the rope barrier. Garth and I got thrust together and up the ramp before landing on the deck relatively unscathed. Above us, we saw a middle-aged woman, clad in black, struggling with a large blue suitcase as she hung onto the guide rope and clambered awkwardly along the side and over people's shoulders. Suddenly the suitcase flew open and its contents, hundreds of thousands of loose wheat seeds, poured out into the sea.

Poor soul, I thought. How distraught she looked. Had she been hoping to use those seeds to sow a crop? Was it meant to feed her family for months? Were they to sell? She was so determined to get on board. Where were the officials? At no point in the crossing were our tickets checked. The seas were so rough I suspect it was too difficult for ticket collectors to access the deck.

No-one we asked could tell us how many hours this trip across the Mediterranean usually took, but your dad predicted that because of the swell it would take much longer than usual. Your dad went to the men's dormitory to lie down, and I went to the crowded ladies' dormitory.

I had bought a cotton sleeping sheet in London to use on hot nights as an alternative to my sleeping bag. I laid it out on my bunk and tried to rest, but twenty minutes after leaving the shore, the ship climbed to the crest of a massive wave, teetered there for a moment, and then plunged to the bottom. My stomach rose and fell with it. I climbed off my bunk and lurched towards the toilet block. The other women, many of whom were wailing as they lay on their beds, didn't look up as I went past. The floor of the toilet block was awash with vomit. When I returned to my bunk, my white sheet had gone.

The women's wailing was unbearable, so I headed outside where I found your dad crouching on the deck. We huddled together for warmth in the face of the bitter wind and stayed like that for the nine hours that it took to reach Beirut. What a relief it was to step onto firm ground. It took a while before the rocking feeling stopped.

* * *

10 December 1971 was a beautiful balmy evening in a peaceful Beirut. I didn't know then that my life would take a 180-degree turn that night. I didn't keep a journal or a diary, so only some details are sharp.

That evening your dad and I sauntered along the shore around the Beirut harbour and port. Our stroll took in the ships and sailing boats moored at the yacht club. It was to be our last evening together after months of being inseparable. Our lives had been fun, with no responsibilities. I didn't want this lifestyle to end.

Beirut was often referred to as the Paris of the Middle East because it was a beautiful city, and after World War I Lebanon had become part of the French colonial empire. We heard a few people speaking French. More women were walking on the streets than there had been in Cairo, and many of them were in western dress.

We enjoyed Beirut's more relaxed atmosphere. As we stood and gazed out to sea, we decided that we should do something special before going our separate ways. Instead of staying at another cheap hostel, where we would be in separate dormitories, we thought we would stay at an upmarket place and have a sophisticated dinner. In all our travelling time together, we had spent money on only bare necessities.

We found a small, elegant old-style hotel in a quiet area. We spoke to the manager, booked a room as a married couple, and inquired if there was a restaurant nearby where the food was good but not too expensive.

The evening unfolded in slow motion. Unhurriedly, we strolled the two blocks to the restaurant recommended by the hotel manager, Garth's arm draped comfortably around my shoulders.

The waiter pulled back my chair, smiling, and brought us the menu. We laughed as we tried to decipher the French and Arabic words to work out what the dishes were. We consulted the waiter, who told us his name was Farouk, and even then we took ages deciding.

With Farouk's help we finally chose falafel with hummus. As the main course, kibbeh, which Farouk explained was Lebanon's national dish comprising mini footballs of beef or lamb with sautéed pine nuts. To accompany this we chose *batata harra*, hot spicy potatoes, and fattoush, a pita bread salad.

We savoured each mouthful, chewing slowly. Eating meat, which we had usually considered too expensive, was a special treat. Your dad, as always, made me laugh with his comments about the restaurant's traditional high-pitched music, over-the-top decor, brightly coloured cushions and large, ostentatious paintings.

The seascape painting reminded us both of the school holidays at the sea we'd enjoyed as children. Garth's parents and his friend Malcolm's had bought a small cottage on the beach at Plettenberg Bay on the South African coast. Your dad told me how he and Malcolm had spent nearly every summer holidaying there, swimming and surfing every day. I described getting badly sunburnt playing beach cricket with my brothers and their friends on the hot sand at Rosebud on the Victorian coast, learning to swim and float, but fearing what might be lurking in the thick mat of green-brown seaweed on the seabed.

Farouk approached the table. 'Have you tried arak?' he asked. 'It's the drink of Lebanon. It's grape juice and aniseed.'

Sipping arak, we ate the last of the fattoush. How good it is to be here, we thought, and smiled, satisfied.

'Would you like a famous Lebanese dessert?' Farouk asked then, as he cleared our empty plates. Your dad and I looked at each other. Were we too full?

'What do you suggest?' Garth asked.

'Mafroukeh is a delicious cake flavoured with orange blossom and with pistachios on top.'

We shared a piece, enjoying the delicate flavours. Our meal had stretched out luxuriously over hours and felt so sophisticated. Tonight, I mused, instead of cheapskate backpackers, we are lovers on a romantic date.

Thanking Farouk, we paid and left, noticing for the first time that we were the only foreigners in the restaurant. With arms entwined, we slowly made our way along the few streets back to our hotel. It was earlier than we'd usually go indoors, but after a chat in the hotel foyer with the manager we slowly climbed the stairs to our room.

The bedroom felt luxuriously spacious and we had it all to ourselves. Through the large window we looked out onto a quiet residential street. There was no mosque, no brothel, no street traders below to disturb the peace. The wide windows had curtains made of thick heavy material, burgundy with a gold embroidered pattern. Garth pulled them across carefully, darkening the room.

I undressed slowly, taking off my shoes and socks, then hanging first my shirt and then my pants over the purple brocade armchair, which looked so Arabic, with silver threads woven through the fabric. I noticed that the whole room smelt deliciously of spices.

Garth turned back the faded red damask bedspread and climbed between the crisp, clean cotton sheets. They were red too. I slipped in next to his warm, welcoming, familiar body. He stroked my neck gently with the back of his hand and spoke tenderly about being together again in Australia. Much later, we fell asleep, and I felt safe in his arms, as I had on every night we had spent together.

9

Separated

The next day I crumpled with sadness as I heard your dad call out, 'I'll see you in Australia.'

His last words at the Beirut airport echoed down the corridor as I watched him disappear. I worried about the dangers he might face backpacking through Afghanistan and Pakistan. I hoped that he and Roslyn didn't get too close, but the smoother their travels went, the earlier he and I would be together again.

I knew that as soon as he called me on his arrival in Australia, wherever I was, I was going to fly home. I wondered when that would be.

I boarded the flight to Nicosia on the island of Cyprus, relieved to have a window seat. It meant I could stare out at the planes on the tarmac with my back turned away from the stranger sitting beside me. I sobbed as quietly as I could, aware that my shoulders were shaking. I felt empty and wondered miserably how I would keep going without Garth next to me. Where was he now? How far had they got into their overland trip?

From Nicosia I caught a bus to Limassol where my cousin George's sister-in-law, Catherine, welcomed me. She was hospitable and kind. I had thought that maybe I'd settle down here for a month or more and get a job, but a few days after my arrival Catherine introduced me to some American friends of hers, Andy and Loris. They were leaving Cyprus to fly to Beirut, then to journey south-east by bus through Lebanon, Syria and Jordan.

They invited me to join them. I'd only been in Cyprus three days but couldn't resist the opportunity to travel to unfamiliar, exotic and potentially dangerous close-by places with this pleasant couple, who were about my age.

Andy and Loris, from San Francisco, travelled like no-one I'd ever seen before. And if you had ever travelled abroad Robbie, I would have recommended that you copy their style.

I always lugged a heavy pack with multiple changes of clothes, a saucepan, stove, plate, cutlery and sleeping bag. They had just a sleeping bag and a small daypack containing the bare essentials, a toothbrush, spare undies, T-shirts, and a bottle of water. Andy had a fat leather wallet crammed full of American dollars. When his old, tattered jeans finally got a hole that was too gaping, he found a shop and bought a new pair, whatever the price.

He and Loris didn't cook their meals from cheap ingredients but went to restaurants to eat. I said I couldn't afford to eat in restaurants, so we compromised and bought cooked food like kebabs and falafels at street stalls.

Together the three of us travelled east, first to Beirut, which stirred mixed memories, then to Damascus, the capital of Syria, and then to Amman, the capital of Jordan.

I remember lots of long bus rides. I missed Garth's shoulder to rest on and the witty quips he would have made as we looked out the window at endless yellow sand and blue sky. But Andy and Loris were easygoing companions who made travelling in these parts of the world feel safer and less lonely, and I liked interacting with the locals we met.

On one particularly long bus ride, while looking out the window I saw way off on the horizon a camel running fast and a man trailing far behind, robes billowing, chasing it. I wondered what the man might be yelling and why the camel was so keen to escape. I can picture you, Robbie, depicting this scene with a pen, capturing the determination of the camel with its haughty, arrogant facial expression and the furious speed and frustration of its owner.

I enjoyed and admired the Arab and local people, but I missed sharing new countries, cultures and experiences with your dad. And at that point, twelve months since leaving home, I wanted a break from travelling.

At the Amman youth hostel, which was situated opposite a mosque and a brothel, several of my fellow travellers and I discussed going to Israel to work on a kibbutz. Like me, they wanted a safe place to settle for a month or so without cost, to experience a different foreign culture.

Everyone agreed that the quickest and cheapest way to enter Israel was by foot across the Allenby Bridge over the Jordan River. But relations between Israel and its Arab neighbours were fragile.

'A soldier shot someone recently crossing that bridge,' Andy said.

A safer way to get there, although more prolonged and more expensive, was to fly from Amman to Ankara, the capital of Turkey, and take another flight to Tel Aviv on the Israeli coast. Andy, Loris and a few others opted for that route. Jake, also an American, and I decided to walk across the bridge.

* * *

The Allenby Bridge was smaller than I expected for a bridge that connected two nations. It was just wide enough for a vehicle to travel one way. But there were no vehicles lined up to cross that day.

A heavily armed guard motioned for us pedestrians to sit on a bench outside the checkpoint. The corrugated iron office had a stack of sandbags beside it. I wondered why they were there.

It was hot, and I soon drank all the water in my bottle. We waited and waited. If Sue had been there with me, we would have taken out our cigarette papers and tobacco. I realised I hadn't smoked while travelling with your dad and no longer thought about smoking, as none of my recent companions smoked either.

I thought how surprised your Grandma and Grandpa would be to learn where I was right now. Sitting and waiting I looked at the Jordan River, so prominent in Biblical stories, but so unimpressive here in its width and its flow. Warmed by the sun, I closed my eyes and daydreamed. I loved swimming in the creeks and rivers near Wandi. A swim would be welcome now to cool off.

'It looks like they are ready for us at last,' said Jake.

He and I had been the only foreigners waiting and were left until last to be processed. A guard waved us inside. There were two desks and two officers. The guard who beckoned to me checked every item in my backpack. He was suspicious about the small gas bottle. After giving him a long explanation about using it for cooking, the other officer studied my passport and papers one page at a time. Finally, he stamped it and let me pass. Soon after, the other guard let Jake go too.

We walked down the wooden bridge towards the Israeli checkpoint. I realised the pile of sandbags were for protection if gunfire broke out between the opposing checkpoint soldiers.

When we reached the other end of the bridge, it was the Israeli officials, also in uniform and heavily armed, who scrutinised the entries on my passport. One of them shot questions at me like bullets from a gun.

'Why did you visit all those Arabic countries? What was the purpose of you going to them? Do you have connections in those countries? Why are you coming to Israel? What is your purpose?'

Hot, tired and thirsty, I was nevertheless careful in the answers I gave. Eventually Jake and I were allowed through and we stepped off the bridge, relieved.

Jake caught a bus to meet someone he knew in Jericho and I found a bus to Tel Aviv. I wondered how far your dad was into his overland journey through Afghanistan. Were he here with me, I bet he'd have walked across the bridge too and delighted in telling me what sort of bridge it was, what load it was designed to take, and all kinds of detail about its construction. And he'd have made me laugh.

10

At the Kibbutz

I was enjoying the freedom of travelling to exotic foreign countries, meeting fascinating people and learning about cultures very different from middle-class suburban Melbourne in the 1950s and 60s, but I was missing your dad. I am sure you would have loved to travel to far off places too, Robbie. I can imagine you making friends wherever you went. You might have sketched people and places, and written insightful stories. I know that you could have kept a more colourful and amusing record than I did.

On a bus to the kibbutz I had booked into, an hour's drive north of Tel Aviv, I plonked down on the only spare seat, nursing my pack. Soon I noticed a frail elderly lady standing. Heaving up my backpack, I offered her my place. She smiled and moved forward just as a burly, young, heavily armed soldier elbowed his way past her and sat down. The old lady and I stood together then, both holding on to the same post for support. I tried to catch her eye, but her face was impassive. There was much more tension here than anywhere else I had seen in the Middle East. Nearly all the young people were in military uniform and wearing a gun.

As soon as I arrived at the kibbutz, which was surrounded by several Arab villages, the volunteers' manager told me that an attack from Lebanon in the north was always a possibility.

Abram, who spoke English with an American accent, showed me the cabin

I would be sharing with two French girls. It was a white, rectangular building. Inside was bare except for three single beds and a kerosene heater. He also showed me the dining room, with long tables and bench seats for communal eating, where we would have our meals, and the storeroom, where he offered me two sets of clothes that I was to wear all the time for work—grey cotton trousers and long-sleeved shirts, and a pair of sturdy brown leather boots.

I was pleased to receive such practical, hard-wearing clothes to wear while working. I could see they would be loose-fitting and comfortable. They were also a welcome change from the clothes I'd been wearing for months.

'Volunteers do outdoor and indoor jobs. Do you have a preference?' Abram asked.

'Outdoors,' I replied without hesitation.

'All right, then,' he said. 'In the morning there'll be a truck to take you to the banana plantation. Be on it at 6.00 am.'

'Can I borrow an alarm clock, please?'

'Ask your roommates to wake you. They're working on bananas too.'

The minute I met Marie and Celeste I discovered that neither spoke English. Here without Sue, I could not rely on her to do the talking. I now had to make more effort.

Slowly, hesitatingly, my school and one-year university French emerged so that when their alarm went off at five-thirty, we got up together, and all staggered out into the cold and dark shivering, before jumping up into the back of the open truck.

There were three other volunteers onboard, two French boys and an American boy from New York. Our supervisor was a gruff Russian man who spoke a little French and a little English.

It was just getting light by the time we arrived at the banana plantation. We unloaded ladders and vast stacks of blue sheaths to protect the unripe bananas from the frost. We worked in pairs, one of us scaling a ladder, the other handing up a sheath, and the one on the ladder wrapping the sheath around the bananas.

The other volunteers were patient when I struggled for words in French, and there was a lot of gesturing and miming. I only realised that someone had told a joke when the others burst out laughing.

We sheathed many green bunches before the scorching morning sun hit and then hopped back onto the truck to return for breakfast.

I sat on a bench at a dining room table with my fellow sheathers and helped myself to plain yoghurt, toast, cream cheese and artificial honey. Were there no bees in Israel?

I felt comfort at being settled in one place with the chance to make friends.

Faye, the Londoner who had driven Sue and me to Ireland, had written to tell me of the kibbutz she was working on, but I discovered it required a three-month minimum stay and I didn't want to commit to so long in one place. I sent her a message with my address.

On my first Saturday, Faye surprised me with a visit. Her kibbutz was only nine kilometres away and she had the use of a car.

It was fun catching up with an oldish friend. We talked and talked, devising a possible plan to travel down Africa together.

It was exciting to think about our next adventure after the kibbutz. I imagined that we would complete the African trip at about the same time Garth arrived in Australia. Faye promised to visit me every week and we'd make definite plans.

A few days after Faye's third visit she slipped and sprained her ankle. With her leg put in a plaster cast, she couldn't drive, so her visits stopped. Detailing our Africa trip was put on hold.

A few Saturdays later, I volunteered to accompany Reuben, the taciturn kibbutz truck driver, on a delivery drive south via Jerusalem to Ein Gedi. I saw it as an opportunity to visit the city that is holy to three major religions, and the famous Dead Sea.

Ruth, a permanent resident who'd become a friend, warned me that Reuben had a reputation with women, so I was wary of him during the long, boring drive.

While Reuben made his first delivery I wandered relaxed around the Jerusalem Arab Quarter, smiling at the traders and locals shopping and bargaining. It was like stepping into a time warp back thousands of years. Had much changed in that time? The food stalls and smells of spices were intoxicating.

After Reuben found me in the market we drove south towards Ein Gedi. Reuben had limited English and hardly spoke a word. He stopped and pointed at the Sea, saying he'd be back for me in a couple of hours while he went to do another delivery.

I was alone on a deserted beach. I picked my way over the hot rocky ground, aware of a sulphur-like smell, then stripped off to my underwear at the water's edge. This deep inland lake stretches across to Jordan, and is too salty for fish to survive.

I put a finger to my lips to test the saltiness. It was indeed much saltier than any sea I'd ever tasted. I tried to swim but couldn't. There was simply too much buoyancy. I tried lying on my back, arms up, and wished I was holding a book, but my legs kept bobbing up higher. It was not as easy as it looks in the photos, but I lay there in the water for ages.

Robbie, I thought about how your Grandpa had taught me to float in Port Phillip Bay at Rosebud, keeping his big rough hand under my back, reassuring me that he would not let me sink, then slipping his hand away without telling me, leaving me to float blissfully by myself.

I would look up into the sky, my body relaxed and my mind peaceful as it was here too, floating on the lowest sea on earth, on the other side of the world. I thought how amazing it was to be having this experience, one that most people would only read about.

I gazed across the water to the far shore of Jordan. I thought about my visit to the ancient city of Petra carved in the sandstone. It had once been a bustling commercial and trading centre on the old Silk Road.

After dreaming and maybe dozing off briefly I realised that Reuben might return soon, so reluctantly waded back to the salty, rocky foreshore, wishing I could wash the salt off my body before dressing, but there was no fresh water there. I sat on a rock and waited for Reuben. Would we have lunch soon? I had assumed we would stop at a cafe on the way down. We had left the kibbutz before the kitchen was open, but we hadn't stopped, so maybe we would on the way back.

A drink would be welcome at least, especially with the salt still on my lips. I thought of how relaxing soaking in the bath at Valerie's had been, after the close shave Sue and I had with the two Belgian men who had given us a lift.

Should I be nervous about Reuben? I wondered. When he finally returned and said we would have to stay the night somewhere, I pleaded with him to drive back to the kibbutz. He protested that it was too far but eventually gave in when I said I had an early morning shift that I mustn't miss.

We arrived back after midnight. I still hadn't eaten or drunk a thing, so no wonder I was feeling nauseous. I collapsed exhausted into bed.

11

Your Beginning Revealed

It was the day after travelling to the Dead Sea that your story starts to emerge, Robbie, but of course I didn't know then that it was you.

I heard Marie and Celeste getting dressed the next morning. I still felt nauseous and, unusually for me, realised I wasn't hungry despite not eating the day before. Perhaps mass-produced food had killed my appetite? I called out to the girls in my best French.

'Tell Abram I'm too tired to work today, please.'

Celeste nodded as she and Marie headed out to the truck. I snuggled back under the blankets and closed my eyes.

I was back floating effortlessly on the salty water of the Dead Sea. It had been such a long way to go there and back in a day. Why didn't Reuben stop to eat or drink? Maybe he had eaten before we set out and had lunch after he dropped me off? No wonder I'd woken up nauseous. I was trying to push my legs under the surface of the water when I heard a loud knocking. A short, dark-haired woman I'd never seen before stood at the door.

'Abram sent me. If you can't go to work, you must see a doctor.'

'I'm not really sick, just tired,' I said.

'It's the rules,' the woman said. 'I'll wait for you to dress and then take you there.'

I gave the doctor the same explanation.

She handed me a specimen jar and pointed to the toilet.

'For a urine sample,' she said.

I came back with the yellow liquid.

'Leave it on the desk. Now, up there,' she said, pointing to the high bed. 'Take off your boots, trousers and shirt.'

After prodding and poking, she looked at me coldly.

'I think you're pregnant.'

I stared at her, afraid. Are you sure? Pregnant? How, when?

My mind flicked back to the last night your dad and I had spent together, that beautiful last evening in Beirut. Garth was who-knows-where in Afghanistan and definitely uncontactable. What would I do? What could I do? Did I want a baby now? A baby? How would I manage with a baby?

The doctor was speaking to me.

'Do you want a baby now?' she asked in the same frosty voice.

'I can't even imagine having a baby,' I spluttered.

Looking at me sternly then, she said, 'There's an abortionist in the nearby town who takes care of pregnant girls from the kibbutz. I will make an appointment for you to see him next week.'

This solution sounded so clinical, clear-cut, pragmatic.

I was in shock. Of course, I had no concept of having a baby in my life just then, or of you as a person, Robbie. It was hard to take in. I didn't feel any different to how I usually did, apart from nausea and fatigue. I simply didn't know what to think. In my mind the future became a tumbled blur.

'Where is the father?' she asked.

Good question, I thought, but right now is it relevant?

During the following week I fretted. Where was your dad? Travelling somewhere out there in the wide blue yonder. I felt utterly alone in trying to work out what to do.

I confided in a South African nurse on the kibbutz. She told me that the surgeon was highly regarded and performed many of these operations for which he was well paid. In seeing my hesitation, she assured me that with this doctor I was in good hands. 'It's the quickest, safest way out of the dilemma, isn't it?' she advised.

But, I asked myself, was an abortion really what I wanted? I was full of fear, shame and dread.

My roommates were fun company, but not confidantes.

While waiting at the abortionist's clinic, I wondered what he'd say. I assured myself that nothing would be done without my agreement. I was in shock and needed more time to think. My mind was a blur. Could I stay on the kibbutz with a baby? Would I be allowed to stay if I can't work? Maybe I could teach English? I would have to learn Hebrew. I thought it unlikely that the kibbutz authorities would kick me out, but if they did, where would I go? My mind was a whirl of scary scenarios. I was contemplating life with a baby, though nothing was clear. How would we manage?

The examination by the doctor, who barely spoke any English, was professional and brief. He took off his gloves and left the room looking concerned, without a word or even a glance in my direction. I got dressed and waited for him to come back. I waited until I realised he was not coming back.

'Well? What did he say?' I asked the clinic receptionist.

'Go back to the kibbutz doctor. She will discuss the result with you.'

I was glad to leave the cold clinic. Back at the kibbutz, the doctor gave me the abortionist's report.

'Even if you want it done, he will not do it,' she said. 'He says it's too late. It's too risky. It's not safe.'

I felt relief and a deep inner happiness. How special this baby must be to have survived the suggested imposition. I felt that both the unborn and I had been looked after. A decision had been made and it was undoubtedly the right one. Now, it was you and me.

The future was still so foggy. I had a major adjustment to make from the carefree wandering lifestyle of the past year, mentally and logistically. I had to try to work out the next step.

Where would we live? Should I enquire about staying on the kibbutz indefinitely? Parents lived separately from their children there. Would I want my baby cared for in the Babies House? And stay in a country where I was a foreigner? Apart from tiredness and nausea I felt fit and healthy. I tried to imagine what my life would be like with a baby but I hadn't grown up around babies, so I really had no idea. In my mind this baby was in the future, a future I could not picture.

But, as I already had a deep sense of us being in the situation together, I was both anxious and optimistic, with no idea how our lives would pan out.

On the first of March, the day after this news, I was cleaning the floor of the children's house when I saw a volunteer walking past with the mail. She handed me a letter stamped from Cyprus. It contained two intimate letters from Garth, which my cousin-in-law Catherine had forwarded on.

One had been written at the beginning of January (two months ago) and the other at the end of January. In the second one your dad wrote how disappointed he had been not to have received a letter from me, but gave me an address and dates when he expected to be in Ceylon (now Sri Lanka).

I was happy that he had written. Should I write to him? What would I say? What could I expect from him when he was so far away? If I wrote telling him my news and the kibbutz address, would it arrive before he left Ceylon? I posted off a brief letter with little hope that he would receive it.

I tried to focus on the present and take it one day at a time until I felt clearer about what to do next. I alternated between feeling excitement and fear about the future.

When I was not with the other girls, my thoughts tumbled all over the place. Who could I share this with? I decided to write to Sue. I knew she was travelling in Europe, so I addressed my letter to Poste Restante, London. Hopefully the postal service would forward it to her current address.

How long would it be before she received it? When she read it, would her reaction be supportive or negative?

Although I knew Sue couldn't solve the situation, it was a relief to share my predicament with a friend. I waited anxiously for her reply.

The doctor informed those in charge of the kibbutz that as I was pregnant they needed to treat me differently.

Celeste asked, 'Why have you moved to ironing instead of working with us on the bananas?' I just shrugged and said they had needed one of us volunteers to do it.

What Abram had said was, 'You'll have to work indoors now.'

'Oh no, I feel perfectly well to work outdoors,' I'd replied.

'You'll start in the ironing room tomorrow for the six-hour shift.'

Judith, a kind, middle-aged, quietly spoken resident, took me inside a small dark room with a tiny window. She showed me the two bins of washed clothes still warm from the dryer and the large ironing board set up beside them.

'It's men's shirts that you'll be ironing,' she said, picking one out. 'Have you ironed men's shirts before?'

'No, I've hardly ever ironed.'

Judith showed me how to spread a shirt over the board to iron first the back, then the sleeves, then the front part with buttons, then the other part with buttonholes, then, finally, the collar.

When I demonstrated to you how to iron your school shirts, Robbie, this was the method I showed you.

Judith said, if I liked, I could sit in a chair to iron, and she showed me the hangers and the rail to hang them. She left the room.

I was grateful to be sitting, but ironing was boring, especially as the shirts were mostly the same colours and patterns. Many were grey like mine, others were blue. They belonged to the supervisors and other men in authority. I only ever ironed men's clothes and wondered who ironed the women's.

Alone for six hours a day without any distractions, I worried, especially when I thought of Australia. Maybe I'd never return. The thought of being exiled from my family's home in Melbourne and our weekender at Wandiligong scared me.

The heat from the iron brought out the smell of the washing detergent and the starch I had to spray on the collars. I tried to remember what it felt like to breathe in the scent of Wandi's peppermint eucalyptus trees. I'd be deeply sad not to smell them again.

Judith came in to see how I was going.

'Very slowly,' I said.

'That's okay, just do them carefully, or there'll be complaints from one or two of the more fastidious men.'

The next day Judith came in to tell me that she had, in fact, had a complaint. A supervisor had told her that his shirt collar was still wrinkled.

I continued wearing my volunteer outfit of un-ironed grey pants and shirts and comfortable boots to walk the five minutes to the ironing room.

One day Judith came in with a basket of fancy dress clothes that residents wanted ironed to wear for Purim. Judith explained that Purim fell on 14 March and was a happy celebration day to commemorate Jews escaping persecution in the Persian Empire around the fourth century BCE.

'There'll be special food too, like pastries, triangular shapes. Kreplachs are filled with minced meat and hamentashen are filled with dates and poppy seeds,' she said.

Judith was excited at the thought of this fun holiday, but I did not share her excitement, even though the festive food she described sounded delicious.

* * *

'Is there another indoor job that I can do where I am not alone?' I asked Abram.

'The only other job is washing dishes,' he said. 'There are two shifts. One is washing the crockery and cutlery from breakfast or lunch. That is six hours. The other is washing pots and pans, and that's four hours. There are two people on each shift. You will alternate shifts each day for variety.'

With a companion to talk to, I won't worry all the time, I thought.

Chatting while washing up did help, though physically I found it more tiring than moving around the banana palms.

If my time off work coincided with Marie's and Celeste's we would go for walks. They both seemed to suspect nothing and their lightheartedness, and the effort of trying to understand and speak French with them, was a welcome distraction.

They had made friends with the two French boys, Fabrice and Pierre, who were part of the banana plantation team. They all wanted me to speak English so that they could improve theirs. On one Saturday, the sabbath when no-one worked, Fabrice suggested we all go frog hunting.

'Where will we find frogs?' I asked.

'Meet us after lunch,' he said.

Even though I was tired and felt like resting, I went with them. We wandered around on the outskirts of the kibbutz grounds, quite a distance from our cabins.

'Where will we find frogs?' I asked Fabrice again.

'Anywhere,' he said. 'Just look in the grass or puddles or drains.'

Like the others, I took off my socks and boots, rolled up my trousers, and waded through the stagnant ponds barefoot.

'I've found two,' yelled Pierre. He picked them up with his hands and dropped them into a metal bucket before tightly securing the lid. Then I saw one in the slime at the bottom of the emptied swimming pool. Fabrice climbed down and after a few attempts managed to scoop the slippery creature out of the green puddle with his hands. Celeste found a few in the long grass. They all ended up in the bucket.

'Would you like to eat them with us tonight in our room?' Pierre asked me.

Ugh, I thought, but I said yes—any distraction from worrying was welcome.

* * *

Walking across to the boys' cabin for dinner, later than we usually ate in the kibbutz dining hall, I was hit by a tantalising aroma of garlic and butter, which I inhaled when I opened the door.

'How did you cook them?' I asked.

'We borrowed a pan from the kitchen,' said Fabrice.

'And some olive oil, garlic and potatoes,' added Pierre.

They'd skinned and cleaned the frogs and fried the legs, balancing the pan over their kerosene heater. They had made fries too. It was the first meal I had eaten for ages that was not mass-produced.

I welcomed a change from yoghurt, cream cheese, dried bean or meat stew, olives and bread, which was healthy and nutritious but monotonous eaten day after day. We ate the legs and fries with our fingers and then licked them clean.

'We're all leaving the day after tomorrow,' Celeste said.

'Oh,' I replied. 'Where will you go?' I felt rattled at the prospect of being alone in the three-bedroom cabin we'd shared since I'd arrived.

'Marie and I are going back to France, and because Fabrice and Pierre are sailors, they are boarding a ship.'

'Where is the ship going?' I asked Pierre.

'We won't know until we're on it,' he replied and laughed.

'Do you smoke?' Fabrice asked me.

'I used to but not for a while,' I said.

'Would you like to try this? Fabrice said. I'd never smoked marijuana before. Pierre made a cigarette, and we each took a puff before handing it on. It was cheap and easy to buy in Israel, someone said. I only had one draw, but it didn't have the uplifting effect I'd expected. The room filled with smoke and I felt drowsy, so I said, 'Merci beaucoup, à bientôt,' and walked wearily to bed.

That night I tossed and turned, overwhelmed by uncertainty. The pregnancy was so unexpected. I knew that this baby, you, was special even though I had no idea of the importance you would play in the future.

In hindsight it's clear that I was being shown how life is unpredictable and sometimes out of our control, and that crucial lessons are learnt from hurdles that we are forced to meet when we find ourselves outside our comfort zone.

Decisions made during those uncertain times were crucial for our future.

My biggest challenge was facing up to a judgmental society that saw pregnancy before marriage as shameful. I now wish that I had not cared so much about others' opinions. But at the time, I was facing an uncertain future in an era of strong moral prejudice. And I felt alone.

Where was your dad? I wished I knew his whereabouts. Would he receive my letter and hear about this unplanned situation?

I had received two welcome letters from him, but I couldn't guess where in the world he was now. If he read my letter he would think I was in Israel, indefinitely. I had shared my secret with Sue, and longed for her reply.

The next afternoon, I was in my room when a resident came to my door and handed me a blue aerogramme. I immediately recognised Sue's distinctive handwriting. I sat on my bed and apprehensively, I tore at the seal.

12

Back to England

Sue's answer was a pivotal moment in our story. It opened a way for you and me to move from the likelihood of living short or long term in the Middle East, however exciting and interesting that may have been.

Sue had replied:

I want to help. I'll be in Switzerland skiing with Chris Newman and his son Timothy between 21 and 24 March. Why don't you join me there? We can drive back to England together if that suits you. Can you fly to Zurich? I'll pick you up at the airport. Reply with details ASAP.

I fronted up to the storeroom to return my kibbutz clothes.

'You can keep the socks and boots,' Abram said.

I was pleased. The socks were woollen and the boots were comfortably worn-in and sturdy. He handed over an envelope with some American dollars, my stipend for the work I'd done. It would cover transport and costs for a day or so. I was grateful. The kibbutz had provided me with food, shelter, and companionship at a time when I needed it the most. *Shalom, Abram, shalom.*

At least now I had a short-term plan. I flew to Zurich from Tel Aviv and searched for Sue in the crowd at the airport, just as I had when I first arrived in London over a year ago.

There she was, waving, this time dressed in a red anorak, white beanie and black knee-high boots. Tears streaming, I hugged her close.

In the car, Sue asked if I wanted to ski. Under different circumstances, I would have jumped at the chance, but not now.

'No, I'll be happy just to sit outside and watch from the balcony,' I said.

My handful of American dollars wouldn't stretch to skiing. I would need to keep my savings for an unknown future.

* * *

It was bliss basking in the peace and fresh air, looking out at the white slopes thick with snow and the colourful figures slaloming down them, calling out to each other. Throughout the day Sue detoured from the ski run for a chat, calling up from the slopes to where I was on the balcony. The snow-topped houses and inns of Verbier with their pitched tiled roofs looked so neat, so perfect.

Remember, Robbie, how your uncle Kim owned a flat at Chamonix in the French Alps, where we expected one day to stay and ski, or for you to practise your rock climbing? Unfortunately, he sold it before we had the chance to go there. But he did have the flat near the start of the chair lift at Mount Buller where you, Jamie and Megan learnt to ski. Grandma bought you all good-quality jackets and pants the second time you went, because the first time you all skied in jeans, T-shirts and jumpers, just ordinary clothes. Remember how wet and cold you got? I remember sitting on a chair lift hearing teenage voices yelling at each other and seeing three boys below going flatout over moguls on a black run. It was you, Jamie and Richard.

At Verbier, Sue was calling me from the balcony for lunch. She, Chris and Timothy would come in from the slopes at midday, and we would share delicious fondues and platters of smoked pork, potatoes and sauerkraut.

I would listen to the lighthearted conversations of the others, and join in, but my anxiety levels rose when alone. But in Australia, I think I would have felt worse, more painfully aware of the harsh judgment passed by society on an unmarried pregnant woman, so I was glad to face this on the other side of the world.

Robbie, you were destined to physically begin in faraway exotic places that one day you might have explored. In these places you would have encountered enormous, dramatic changes in your lifetime. Beirut, that beautiful city of your dad's and my romance has since experienced disasters.

On the Channel trip, the closer we got to England, the darker the shadow of the unknown became. I dreaded anyone asking what I was going to do in the future because I had no idea, and saying anything out loud about it only highlighted my predicament to myself. What was I to do? Where would I find somewhere to live, to work? Might I return to live at the kibbutz? Spend the rest of my life ironing clothes or washing dishes for others? Nothing was clear.

Back in London Sue insisted I stay with her in the small flat she had rented in Earl's Court, after leaving Nevern Mansions months earlier.

'Do you think I should contact Helen and John Stewart?' I asked her.

'You need friends. You liked them and they were caring towards you. Ring them.'

Your dad's godparents had been friendly and hospitable to me before we left. But was I brave enough to face a couple who in South Africa had been so close to Garth's parents? Perhaps I could just visit them and not mention the pregnancy. Sue urged me to call them.

'If I tell them what's happened, they might want nothing to do with me?' I wondered aloud, worried.

'Then that would be their loss,' Sue said. 'You have nothing to lose by contacting them.'

I rang and briefly spoke to Helen, just telling her that I was back in London. She invited me over for lunch that Sunday.

13

Amazingly Reunited

It was the end of March 1972 when I visited the Stewarts again. Over succulent roast lamb, Helen and John asked about my recent travels. They were both interested in the countries I'd visited and my kibbutz experience.

After lunch, John went to his study and Helen and I moved into the lounge room. Helen looked straight at me and asked me directly why I was back in England. I blurted out that I was pregnant, and she without hesitation said, 'And Garth is the father.'

She was obviously concerned as she called John in from the next room and told him.

After a moment's silence, John said, 'Garth must be told.'

'But I don't know where he is,' I said, bursting into tears. 'I don't even know what country he's in. I will only know when he gets to Australia and contacts me.'

John quizzed me about where I had seen Garth last and where he was headed then and what date that was and where was he going after Afghanistan and when had I received letters from him on the kibbutz and had they been delivered via the London Poste Restante? When and from where had I written to him?

With scant information John set out to achieve what I considered impossible. He asked me to call him in a week. What made him so confident? Where would he begin the search? I thought your dad would never be found, at least not before late September, when our baby was due. Perhaps your dad would never know about you, our baby. Would it matter if he never knew? How ironic if I remained in England permanently and he stayed in Australia. But one step at a time, I reminded myself.

Meanwhile, I needed to earn some money, so I applied to register with an employment agency.

A fair-haired woman with a pleasant face was sitting at a desk neatly stacked with folders. She took down my details and said, 'Sit at that typewriter and copy this paragraph.'

'I can't type,' I said.

'You must do the test.'

'I can't type.'

'To register with the agency, it is a requirement that you copy this paragraph,' she said calmly, standing beside the typewriter.

I concentrated and stared at the machine, studying the alphabetic order on the keyboard and, using just one finger, pushing down on each letter. *Tap.* Another. *Tap.*

I didn't make any mistakes, but, by the time the woman came over to see what I had done, I had only completed two lines of a ten-line paragraph.

'Hmm,' she said, looking first at the page in the typewriter and then at me. 'Can you do shorthand?'

'No, I'm better with figures,' I said.

She sent me to a large accountancy firm. It was an open office with desk space for each office assistant. Janey, the supervisor, put some pages with columns of figures on my desk.

'Just add them up and let me know when you've finished,' she instructed.

I soon discovered that Janey was overwhelmingly kind but also hard-working and stressed, probably because the other office girls were laid-back and slow. In the mornings they would struggle in, then head to the ladies' room to apply their makeup and chat. They wouldn't have done much work by the time the morning tea trolley came around. I didn't feel like joining in on their gossip, so I kept my head down.

A week after first telling the Stewarts, I phoned them again.

'Come for Sunday lunch,' said Helen. 'John has news for you.'

John never explained how he did it and I was in too much shock to persist in an answer, but he had tracked your dad down in an ashram in India. John said Garth already knew about my pregnancy, because the day before he had received my kibbutz-addressed letter, but had no idea until John's call that I was back in England.

I had thought about your dad almost every day since we had parted, but everything was different now. So it was with a mixture of relief, delight and anxiety that I listened as John told me a few days later that he had spoken to Garth on the phone and Garth was returning to England as soon as he had sorted out transport. At least he hadn't set off to be with me in Israel, which was a relief.

I was grateful for Helen and John's concern and help but I wished I had been the one to talk to Garth on the phone.

'What will Garth's parents think about this? Will you tell them?' I asked Helen and John.

'They will not approve, but don't worry, we won't be telling them,' John said.

Nine days later, I was at my desk adding up a long column of numbers when Janey told me that John Stewart had called, asking for me to phone him.

'It must be important for someone to phone here,' Janey said. 'You can use the phone in my office if you like.'

Slowly, I dialled the Stewarts' number. John answered.

'Hullo, Margaret. Garth has been in touch. He has made good time and is arriving at Paddington Station tomorrow at 11 am. Do you want to meet him there?'

'Of course I will,' I said. 'And thank you.'

Janey was dismayed when I said I was handing in my notice, effective immediately. She asked if I couldn't finish the week out, but I said, 'No, sorry,

I had to leave at the end of the day and I would not be back tomorrow.' She kindly said that I would be welcome back if I needed a job in the future.

The next morning on the train to Paddington I felt nervous, excited at the thought of being with Garth again, but also wondering if his presence would solve anything. How would our relationship be after the separation and the dramatic change in circumstances? I was taking nothing for granted.

At Paddington, I stared at the hundreds of commuters as they hurried to and from so many different platforms. Would we ever find each other in this crowd? I found the platform where his train would arrive. The air was hot and heavy with cigarette smoke which made me feel nauseous. The loudspeaker blared out train changes.

I spotted a familiar though bedraggled, bearded, long-haired fellow with a huge, dirty pack on his back. We made eye contact at the same moment. I felt a surge of excitement. Standing there was the man who had filled my thoughts for months, in front of me, in the flesh—your dad. I also felt an overwhelming sense of relief.

We approached each other shyly and hugged and kissed each other on the cheek. I knew it was essential to take things moment by moment. I had no idea what Garth was feeling about this new situation. One step at a time, I reminded myself.

We were quiet on the Tube to Earl's Court and the walk to Sue's flat. Garth was tired after a week of travelling on trains and buses and hitchhiking. Talking about our adventures since we'd been together could wait.

I'm relieved to say, Robbie, that within hours of meeting up again, Garth and I had happily settled into our former intimacy. That night in bed, nestled in his arms, I thought how amazing this outcome was after months of anxious uncertainty.

* * *

Now we had to work out what steps to take. Just like me when I had first got the news on the kibbutz, your dad wanted to take things slowly. It was too soon, he said, for him to make any commitment. We couldn't stay at Sue's flat indefinitely, and Garth said he didn't want a permanent engineering job yet, but he needed to earn money.

As it turned out, within three days we had an answer.

Sue told Chris Newman that we needed somewhere to live and that Garth needed work. Chris said he needed a capable person to build a conservatory on the back of his house. So that is how we came to live at your first address, Robbie, one that I thought sounded so quintessentially English: Arbour House on Hemp Lane in Wigginton, near Tring, Hertfordshire.

To get there, Garth and I travelled for forty-five minutes northwest of London by train until we arrived at Tring Railway Station. From there, in Chris's car, we drove along narrow roads passing small green fields with copses of elms, beeches and huge oaks, and through a tiny village, until we pulled into the wide driveway of a picturesque white two-storey house in a spacious garden. We sat in the drawing room with Chris and Tricia and discussed the build over tea while their three-year-old daughter, Claire, played with blocks in the corner.

'The baby's asleep,' Tricia said. 'He's four months.'

'You must know a lot about babies,' I said.

'I'm still learning,' she said, laughing. Tricia seemed laid-back but efficient, as evidenced by the clean, tidy house.

'If Garth works here, where would we live?' I asked.

'Come and see.'

They led us out towards the bottom of the deep back garden where there was a long, dirty-white caravan. It looked as though it had always been there.

'Chris bought it years ago but found it too big and heavy to tow, so it just sat here, ready for you.' Tricia smiled. 'You can live here during the construction. Have a look inside. What do you think?'

At one end of the interior was a single bed that doubled as a couch, and at the other end was a second, wider bed. Between stood a kitchen area complete with a tiny gas stove with two hot plates and a sink.

'We haven't used it for years,' Tricia said. 'I'll sweep and clean it out if you decide to live here. But there aren't the spiders and cobwebs that you'd find in Australia.' She laughed. Tricia was pleasant and easygoing. I guessed that she was about eight years older than me.

'It looks fine,' I said. 'I've never lived in a caravan before.'

An offer of a year-long job with free accommodation seemed too good to refuse. Immediately, I thought, it would solve a lot of problems, especially for the baby and me.

'We'll ring you tomorrow and let you know our decision,' said Garth.

14

In the Caravan

After discussing the Newmans' proposal overnight, Garth and I decided to accept it. Garth wasn't sure about working at the conservatory for a year. I could tell he was still restless.

When we returned two days later the caravan looked inviting, nestled under the spreading branches of a tall elm in the bottom corner of the garden. Its two metal steps vibrated as Garth and I stepped up with our backpacks.

To me, the best feature was the view through the windows. On one side we looked out at flowering mustard fields of brilliant yellow with a copse of beech trees beyond. On the other side two brown-and-white Clydesdales were grazing contentedly on the thick green grass. These views made our limited living space feel more expansive. The Newmans' residence, Arbour House, was barely visible through the trees in the garden, so that even with the curtains open, we were private. I grinned at Garth, and we hugged each other.

'*Knock, knock*, can I come in?' Tricia called.

'Of course,' we said.

Tricia came in with her arms around a heavy-looking cardboard box.

'Here is a set of sheets, some pillow slips and some blankets. It's enough for now but I'll bring over more as the nights get colder. Also, here are a couple of cups and a teapot, two small saucepans and a frying pan. Yell out if there's anything else you need.'

She deposited the box on the single bed. We thanked her.

Being with your dad, more or less settled in our own place and financially secure, at least for the near future after months of fear and uncertainty, was for me hard to believe. It was so good to be sharing the pregnancy, even if just for the short term.

My fear about how I would manage when our baby was born was always there though, lurking beneath the surface. It lessened as I focused on living in the present with your dad, who I loved being with every day.

Garth started working enthusiastically on the project Chris had outlined. Initially Chris worked alongside him, but quickly realised that Garth could solve whatever problems arose. Your dad had never built anything before. His civil engineering degree meant that he could read architectural drawings and knew how to adjust them if necessary. Sometimes Chris disagreed with him, but your dad would always argue his point calmly and often convinced Chris to his way of thinking. The conservatory was to be an elegant, attractive addition to the drawing room.

'It will be lovely to sit in during sunny days, or rainy days, warm, reading a book or having lunch,' said Tricia. 'Many people we know are building a conservatory. It's quite the fashion.'

At morning tea break and lunchtime, if the weather was fine, we often sat in the garden with Tricia and Chris too, if he was not travelling abroad. The men usually talked about the job. Tricia and I talked about the plants in the garden, her background in New Zealand, my life in Australia, and recipes, especially vegetarian ones now that Garth, after his trip to India, was no longer eating meat.

Chris and Tricia invited us to use their guest bathroom, so each evening your dad and I would go into the house together to share warm soapy water in the large bath upstairs.

Sue visited us soon after our move to Hemp Lane. She stayed a few nights, sleeping in the single bed.

'You can't live in a caravan on the outskirts of a wee village miles from a train station without a car,' she said. 'Especially with a baby on the way. How will you get to the hospital?'

Sue was fiercely financially independent and had never asked her parents back in Australia to tap into her savings before, but she did now, to buy a car for Garth and me.

The car made a huge difference to us—the blue Beetle that your dad and Chris chose from a secondhand dealer near Tring gave us independence and freedom. Within a week of making this generous gift, Sue returned to Australia to attend her brother's wedding, at which she met her future husband, Gerald.

I drove the Beetle to the Tring farmers' market for fresh vegetables, which were the basis of our every meal. Cooking meat-free dishes with the aid of a vegetarian cookbook I found in the Tring bookshop wasn't easy for me. I started with simple meals which still took hours to prepare.

As a child, Robbie, I'd watched Grandma cook meals. Seemingly with little effort, she presented a two-course meal for five every night, except Sunday.

'I have Sunday night off,' she'd say. 'We can eat leftovers.'

Grandpa grew most of the vegetables, and his suburban orchard produced fruit for apple and rhubarb crumble or peach pie, or stewed plums. I think Grandma enjoyed cooking more than I did. You always glowingly praised her meals.

At the local farmers' market I would buy a box of potatoes, muddy as the grower's gumboots, hauled into the boot of our Beetle straight off the back of his truck.

'Dug this morning,' the farmer would say cheerily.

A bunch of spring greens—the dark-green loose leaves of young cabbages, freshly picked and still wet with dew—only cost ten pence. I would include them in several meals, raw or steamed. It was plain English fare but your dad always made positive remarks about the food I put in front of him at lunch and dinner, which I found encouraging.

At the market, my secret treats were the meat pies or occasionally the blackcurrant tarts straight from the vendor's oven, that I would eat hot on the spot. Your dad would see me arrive home, attempting to lug in the week's shopping, take one look at my face and ask, 'What have you been eating this time?' I'd quickly wipe the sauce or jam off my mouth.

He would help me unload the car before wandering back over to the construction site which was only forty metres away.

On Sundays, Garth's day off, we always drove somewhere. The countryside and its villages offered scenes straight out of my childhood storybooks. So I spotted the steeple The Flying Postman came to grief on and the wood near Milly-Molly-Mandy's thatched cottage. Little Friend Susan's house had to be nearby, and Billy Blunt's too. Your dad always looked puzzled when I pointed these things out.

For my birthday in July, he gave me a beautifully illustrated hard copy of Kenneth Grahame's *The Wind in the Willows*, a book I loved and one he also had read in South Africa.

'Would you like to do something special for your birthday?' he asked.

'I'd love to go punting on the river at Oxford,' I said.

So we did. How romantic it felt gliding along with me relaxing at the back of the punt while Garth stood and propelled us rhythmically through the still water. Iridescent male mallards and white swans on the river and the weeping willows reaching over from the bank made it a quintessentially English day out.

Every few weeks I would send a postcard to your Grandma and Grandpa, Robbie, depicting a famous English building or a landscape. I'd write describing the beautiful countryside surrounding where we were living. I told them nothing about who I was living with or that I'd stopped travelling or the challenges and changes in my life. I wasn't going to worry them when there was nothing they could do, on the other side of the world, to help. Telephoning then was very expensive. We never once spoke on the phone in the years I was away.

One day Garth and I decided to visit a village called Chesham. On the way we travelled roads so narrow that passing cars needed to drive sheer to the thick hazel hedgerow on their left. There was a beautiful old stone gatehouse at the entrance to an estate and a grand drive leading to a castle. But the main attraction of Chesham for me was a shop selling mushy peas pies, especially as by this stage I was finding it challenging to produce a nutritious vegetarian meal every day. These pies were a pastry shell filled with mushy peas, covered in mashed potato and then topped with gravy. We sat in a park under a spreading horse-chestnut tree and ate them. They were delicious.

As my pregnancy advanced, the autumn nights brought heavy frosts and occasionally snow. I would still be warm under the blankets when Garth dressed for work. The windows of our caravan would be all iced up on the outside and sometimes on the inside too. Garth would hand me a cup of steaming tea before cooking porridge for our breakfast. I would wipe the window clear and watch him as he stepped outside into the cold, rubbing his hands together to keep them warm. His anorak now doubled as his work jacket, but he didn't wear gloves. Clean-shaven now, he no longer had warmth from a beard. At night, with the radiator on, our small space soon became cosy. At bedtime, I drifted off to sleep, warm and nestled in his arms.

15

Making the Right Decision

We'd been living in the caravan for nearly three months when Tricia suggested that I register at the local hospital where she had had her babies and where I would be going for the birth. This, Robbie, is when I felt keenly the relentless pressure of a judgmental society. It was never you that was the problem but my acceptance of the shame imposed and the way this confused my thinking.

Looking back now, I wish I'd resisted the pressure from the beginning and thought more of the wonder of having a baby, but at the time I didn't realise how miraculous and life-changing that would be. And a future with my baby, you, was still so unclear. I could not see an immediate way forward.

At the hospital, I was interviewed by a staff member, maybe she was a nurse, who, once she had taken down my details, quizzed me.

'Are you married?' she asked.

'No.'

'Are you getting married before the baby is born?'

'No.'

'A baby of an unmarried woman is nearly always given up for adoption. We can help you with that.'

I said nothing.

'Do you want to sign a form now to say that you will agree to give the baby up for adoption at birth?'

'No.'

'What are your plans for yourself and the baby after birth?'

'I don't have any plans.'

'How will you look after a baby?'

'I don't know.'

'If you don't sign the adoption papers beforehand, you'll sign them in the hospital. It is easier if you sign them now.'

'I won't sign them now.'

Two weeks after I visited the hospital I had a surprise visit from a tall, prim, middle-aged woman who'd been alerted by the hospital to talk about my baby's future. She was neatly dressed in a straight skirt and plain grey blouse. Her hair was in a bun. She wore no makeup.

I invited her into the caravan and she looked around carefully before sitting down on the single bed, our couch. Thank goodness I had made the bed that morning and done the dishes. Not that it was any of her business, but I felt under scrutiny and that my housekeeping was part of her test.

'This first visit is just to introduce myself,' she said in a pleasant voice. 'I want to explain how my visits are to help both you and the baby's father. I also help adoptive parents find suitable babies. On my next visit, which will be in two weeks, I need to talk to the father too. Can he be here?'

'I'll ask him,' I said.

That night Garth and I discussed her visit.

'I can't take time off work to talk to her,' he said firmly.

'I've already told her that you don't want a baby or to get married, but she wants to hear it from you. If you see her once, that should be enough.'

In describing her to your dad, I called her The Official Lady—TOL for short—but she was a social worker, also known as a "moral worker" in some official documents. What, I wondered, did she mean when she said her visits were to help me?

Every day in the caravan, Robbie, I felt a mixture of delight at being settled with your dad, gratitude that my immediate needs were being cared for and anxiety about what would happen after our baby was born. Just as I had pondered whether the kibbutz where I had been living would expel me once I had a baby, I wondered how your dad would be. His certainty about not wanting a baby increased my uncertainty. How would it be resolved? In the meantime, Sue's gift of the Beetle made everyday activities unrestricted and added a fun element to our lifestyle.

'Where will we go tomorrow?' Garth asked on his Sunday off, looking at our map of Hertfordshire. 'How about Aldbury?' he said. 'Apart from Wigginton, it's the closest nearby village we haven't visited yet.'

After the signpost announcing Aldbury, we found the village green with its whipping post, stocks and duck pond. It all looked so calm and peaceful now but I pitied the accused witches whom the villagers had dunked here—innocent if they drowned, guilty if they survived—and thieves on their knees, with their heads locked in the stocks so that the other villagers could pelt them with rotten fruit or vegetables.

There were two pubs, the Valiant Trooper and the Greyhound. It was at the Greyhound on Stocks Road, right opposite the village green, when suddenly we heard music and saw a group of well-built, burly men dancing on the pavement.

Curious, we wandered over and joined the onlookers. One musician was playing the melodeon and another a fiddle. Bells on the dancers' shoes jingled in time to the music.

'Who are they?' I asked a local standing next to me.

'Our footy team,' he said. 'They are Morris dancing. They'll pass around a hat soon, then go inside to drink the takings.'

We went into the pub and had a beer. It was served warm, so unlike the cold beer I was used to drinking in Australia, but a reminder of the beer in the chasers your dad had introduced me to in Scotland.

The atmosphere in the cosy lounge was celebratory. The footy team had won and the players were in high spirits. Your dad pointed out two players who were still dancing outside, and we laughed. At that moment, I felt lighthearted, happy, as if I didn't have a care in the world.

But on the drive home, I felt a tightness in the pit of my stomach. Tomorrow TOL would be visiting again and this time she was going to talk to Garth. It was a feeling like returning for a new school year after a long summer holiday, only worse.

I sat in the garden with Tricia and Claire while TOL spoke to Garth in the caravan. He emerged looking serious.

'Your turn,' he said.

He was looking at the ground as he walked past, giving nothing away in his expression as he headed back to work.

I greeted the social worker. She looked pleased and said, 'It's clear from talking to Garth that he doesn't want to get married before the birth of the child, and he doesn't want to keep the baby.'

'Yes, I know.'

'You realise you have no option but to give the baby up for adoption.'

I stayed silent.

She continued. 'The sooner you sign papers the better. Then we can arrange a suitable match. I will find a couple that has a similar education and background to you and Garth. Would you like to sign the handover papers today?'

'No.'

She told me to think seriously about what she had said then left saying she would be back in two to three weeks.

16

What Is Best for You?

Even when I only knew you as the baby to be born, Robbie, I always wanted what was best for you. The struggle I faced was knowing what was best. It was a conflict between the pressure of advice from TOL—who sounded so authoritative with her well-practised argument that I was being selfish if I didn't do what she said was best for the baby—and my maternal instinct.

At each visit, TOL reminded me about decisions that had to be made "sooner rather than later". She left papers regarding relinquishing the baby and urged me to sign them. It would be better for all concerned, she argued.

I was continually asking myself, what will I do when the baby is born? I felt cowardly when I thought of facing people I'd known, especially if I returned to Australia. But, I thought, would my embarrassment at being unwed override my innate desire to be a mother now?

I had seen a pregnant, unmarried girl experience stigma in Australia. A fellow history student at Monash University in the mid-1960s would turn up to tutorials with her increasingly protruding belly. About a week before her baby was due she invited me to her wedding. There was only a handful of guests.

'What about your parents?' I had asked.

'They've disowned me,' she had said with tears in her eyes.

I thought how brave she was and decided I couldn't ever be as courageous as her. Not that I thought for a moment that my parents, who were kind and loving, would disown me, or a baby. My worry in England was rather that if I gave the baby up for adoption, how would my parents feel about the loss of their first and longed-for grandchild? That is, if I ever told them and if I ever returned to Melbourne. But losing me to the other side of the world would make them sadder than any alternative. And mostly, how would either decision affect the baby? Would it have lifelong effects on the little person inside me, soon to emerge? These were the questions, Robbie, that kept going around in my head.

TOL tried to be friendly, but I saw her as the enemy. She wanted to make me face up to what would be happening in a couple of months, she said. She demanded clear-cut answers which I couldn't give.

'There's no question about it,' she repeated, but more gently this time. 'You must adopt the baby out. It is selfish and unfair on the babe for you to think about keeping it. Don't you want the best for your baby?'

Of course, I wanted what was best for my baby. But did I believe that a married couple would be better parents for my child than me, even if I were a single mum? Your dad was a few years younger than me, and I understood his reluctance to take on fatherhood at the time.

I had to live with this decision for the rest of my life. But how could I support a baby on my own? My teacher qualifications and experience would help me to get a job in the UK, but I would have to figure out a way both to work and to look after the baby. Right now I couldn't think of a way to do it.

The pressure to adopt out was intensified closer to the birth date. TOL argued her case as if there was only one course of action. It felt like she was treating my baby like a commodity, which was ignorant and cruel. How could I contemplate giving away my own baby? This baby might be the only one I ever have. Would the child feel in its life that it had been unwanted and abandoned by its birth mother, rejected, to be given away to strangers? Would the child later say, what was wrong with me that my mother gave me up?

TOL wanted my agreement, at the latest, by the time I arrived at the hospital. I felt an urgency to decide before going into labour. Tricia had lent me a book about babies. In it I read that the healthiest start a baby could have is to be breastfed.

So at TOL's next visit I told her, 'I do want this baby to have the very best in life.' She looked pleased and visibly relaxed. 'So I've decided to breastfeed the baby. I've read that it gives a baby the healthiest start.'

'For how long?' she asked, startled. 'That is not a good idea. You are far less likely to give the baby up after breastfeeding, and I already have a couple lined up. They are excited at the prospect of adopting your baby, but it needs to be immediately after birth. That will make for a clean break which will be better for you so you won't form any attachment to the baby. The sooner the adoptive parents have the baby, the quicker they can form an emotional bond.'

'How soon after the birth?' I asked, stunned. It was the first time I'd heard that a specific married couple was waiting for my baby.

'It will go to them straight after it's born.'

'I've read that babies should breastfeed for at least the first three months,' I said. 'That's what I'll do, breastfeed for three months. That will give me experience with a baby and to realise the best long-term solution.'

She would not give up so easily.

'You are confused. The respectable couple I have lined up is not only preparing the room for the baby's immediate future, but they also have the means to support its upbringing. Would you want to deprive the baby of a financially supported life?'

I was grateful that I was older, Robbie, more mature than many younger girls, some still teenagers, who found themselves in this dilemma. I was also blessed with support from friends. My determination would have been much harder without the care and friendship of the Stewarts and the Newmans whose moral backing gave me more confidence in grappling with the pressure.

I loved being with your dad, who was providing us with daily security. He had abandoned his footloose and fancy-free travelling lifestyle and offered love, comfort and the stability I needed to work out the best solution for you.

Younger girls about to have a baby out of wedlock faced a cruel outcome at the end of their pregnancy. I alternately felt scared and blessed. They would mostly have felt fear and sadness, even lifelong grief and guilt.

I refused to dwell on what might happen after the first three months were up. Excitement overcame most of my former anxiety. I didn't know anything about labour, the birthing process or babies, but I took advice from Tricia. She recommended that I take some prenatal classes at the hospital.

It all seemed straightforward, I thought. Giving birth wasn't going to be too hard. I'm fitter than some of those other women, I thought. I'll sail through it.

'Fathers are allowed to attend the birth now,' the midwife had explained, 'but most don't.'

When I got home, I asked Garth if he would be with me at the birth.

'Of course I will if you want me there,' he said.

'You'll have to attend some antenatal classes to learn how to help during the labour.'

'Okay,' he said, nodding in agreement.

I smiled happily and hugged him.

17

Your Arrival

Despite my decision, TOL did not give up. With the birth imminent she came trying to persuade and cajole, showing me forms to sign and pointing at a dotted line. She asked for Garth to be present too so that she could quiz him again about his attitude and intentions. She spoke to him in private. Garth's reason for not meeting with TOL at every visit was genuine. He didn't want to take so much time off work. Sometimes he asked me to be his trade assistant.

'Can you climb up the ladder and hold down this iron bracket while I go to town for a drill bit?' he asked me one morning.

'Well, okay, but don't be too long,' I said. 'TOL is coming to see me today. What if she arrives and finds me perched on the roof?'

I slowly climbed the ladder with my bulging belly, anxiously eyeing the distance to the ground. It was challenging to get comfortable up there on the sloping surface, but I plonked down heavily on a tile and pressed my hand firmly on the place Garth indicated.

The Beetle roared off down the driveway. Tricia came out to hang washing on the line and spotted me.

'What on earth are you doing up there?' she said. 'You shouldn't be on the roof in your condition. What is Garth thinking of?'

It was a relief to see the Beetle return. Garth helped haul me up and with him holding my hand I tentatively negotiated the ladder's rungs.

Back on the ground, we laughed. I loved the fact that life with your dad was never boring and that, despite my bulge, I was fit and agile enough to cope with his requests. I was chuffed to be his assistant.

TOL did arrive later that morning and told me that as the birth was so close it was vital for me to look after myself. Your dad and I chuckled at the thought of her seeing me up on the roof.

The nurse who examined me when I first booked into the hospital had guessed a date. About 15 September, she said. I had guessed that conception was in Beirut about two weeks before Christmas. This date made sense.

Tricia called in to check on me every morning after the fifteenth and declared each day that the baby was late.

The birth seemed imminent after intermittent contractions started early on 19 September but became more consistent by late morning. Without a clue as to how quickly a baby could be born, and with us being half an hour to an hour's drive from the hospital, depending on traffic, we decided we would go when my contractions became stronger and more regular.

It was 10 am. Tricia agreed when we asked her for advice.

At the hospital, many, many hours of intense contractions followed. Garth massaged my tummy and lower back. At the antenatal class he'd attended with me he had learnt this technique.

It was now 4 am on 20 September, and I was so tired and the sensation of the severe tightness and pain was so scary, that I accepted the gas mask the midwife offered me. That's when I called Garth, who was there by my side, Richard Attenborough. Garth told me this afterwards, a bit offended, but I had no recollection of it. The gas was affecting me, but was it helping?

'Push, push hard,' said the younger midwife, whose name was Julie.

'There's the head. We can see the top of the head,' said the older one, Sheila.

'Big push, now shallow breathing, now, pant, pant, baby's coming,' Julie said excitedly, then she went quiet. I heard a soft muttering between them.

Garth gently unclasped my hand, which he had been holding throughout most of the labour, and stood watching as the baby emerged.

Then we heard it, that magical cry of a newborn's first breath. Everyone relaxed, and the midwives laughed. I looked at Garth. His face looked crumpled, and his eyes were full of tears.

'You have a baby boy,' said Julie, showing him the little body. Garth looked at it in amazement.

'Was there a problem?' I asked.

'The umbilical cord was wrapped twice around baby's neck,' Sheila said. 'We had to work quickly to untangle it. We could have called a doctor, but we managed.'

Robbie, you won't be surprised that the nurses exclaimed that your head was much bigger than they'd expected. It explains your struggle to find a Knox boater big enough.

Then Julie, holding the bloody, purple little body closer to me, said, 'We'll weigh baby then clean him up and bring him back in a tick.'

My sense of exhilaration exploded with you in my arms, all cleaned up and wrapped in a white waffle blanket. How beautiful you looked, how perfect and calm, I thought, staring at you.

You, wide-eyed, stared right back at each person in the room, fixing each of us with a steady gaze, first pausing at me, then your dad, then Sheila and Julie, then the doctor and finally the nurse. It was as if you were committing each face to memory. No effect from the recent drama of your birth showed in your expression, only calm intelligence.

'He weighs eight pounds, and it was certainly time he came out,' Julie said. 'See, his fingers and toes are wrinkled, like when you've been in a bath too long.'

I could only see perfection and continued gazing at you in awe. Nothing else had ever come close to the wonder of holding you and the joy of looking at you for the first time.

We had been together, Robbie, only nine months, but already you had taught me so much and shown that we were meant to be together. You had survived the possible kibbutz drama and the relentless onslaught of a government agency. We were together because it was destined that way.

How lucky I am to have been given such a gift as you and that you were determined to be that gift.

Excited but exhausted, your dad drove back to Wigginton. I'd lost track of time, but think it was about 4.30 in the morning. He needed to sleep and to tell Tricia and Chris the news. A nurse supported me on each side and led me to a dormitory-type ward of nine other new mothers.

While I was in the labour ward I heard screaming from another room.

'Who's that?' I had asked a nurse.

'It's a girl who is terrified. She's on her own. Adoptive parents are here ready to take her baby immediately after the birth.'

My heart went out to this girl. There were no social benefits for single mothers. If her family refused to have their daughter and child, they had little or no option but to give the baby up for adoption.

I felt so fortunate that I was already definite about my baby and me facing the world together. One moment I felt confident but at other moments I wondered how on earth we would manage. Right now, I decided that I would concentrate on giving you the best first three months I could. There was a lot to work out, but not today. There were practical skills like breastfeeding and nappy changing to master first.

Eventually I drifted off to sleep, deaf to the sounds of the other girls. I was feeling wrapped in love and gratitude and amazement.

After sleeping for hours, I awoke when a nurse came across the ward to me. 'Does baby have a name yet?' she asked.

'No,' I answered, suddenly sad. It hadn't seemed appropriate with so much uncertainty before the birth to think about a boy or girl's name.

'We're opening the door for the visiting hour in five minutes,' the duty nurse announced, striding the full length of the ward. All of us new mums sat up. Some brushed their hair, others looked in a compact mirror, pursed their lips and carefully applied lipstick and dabbed their cheeks with powder. When the door opened, there was a crowd of men waiting outside, each one jostling to get in first, and I felt a surge of excitement at the prospect of seeing your dad again.

All the men filed in and went to their wives. Every bed had a visitor except mine. Half an hour passed and my tears welled up. Some of the men started to leave. Now that the baby was born, had Garth abandoned us?

Then I looked up to see his handsome face next to the bed. I waited for an explanation for his lateness, but instead he said, 'I think we should get married.'

Startled, I searched his face.

'Are you sure?' I asked.

'Yes, I'm sure.'

'I am not giving the baby up for adoption,' I said.

'Of course not,' he replied.

It sank in slowly. I remember reclining back into the big hospital pillow. Tears flowed as your dad went to look at you, his baby son, in the nursery. I had not wanted Garth to feel under any pressure to marry. Now his decision was unexpected but welcome, because Robbie, you, our special, precious baby and your dad, my closest friend, and I had become a family.

My shame at having a baby before marriage was still below the surface, but under the circumstances there could not have been a happier outcome. Your dad came back from the nursery. I smiled as he hugged me before hurrying off. Visiting hours were over and he had a wedding to organise.

Tricia visited the next day. She was happy for us all, Garth, the baby and me, and said she'd hoped for our marriage all along.

'You are such close friends,' she said. 'Chris and I are not at all surprised.'

'He was late to visit yesterday,' I told her.

'Ah, that's because he wanted to talk to Chris and me about organising the wedding.'

TOL also visited me in the hospital, which was unwelcome. She was surprised about this unexpected turn of events, but still, she didn't give up.

'I'll visit again when you are back in the caravan,' she said. 'The difficulties of your situation might be clearer then. I'll come to make sure that neither Garth nor you have changed your mind. The couple hoping for your baby is still preparing for his delivery to them. I've told them you've had a boy. They'll be disappointed if they can't adopt him.'

Well, tough, I thought.

I do wonder what you would have thought when I told you all this, Robbie. I'm not sure if you would have laughed or cried or both. Or, maybe you would have been pleased to have such an interesting background to your birth and beyond? Certainly, you would have had a lot to ponder on what might have been. Or, perhaps you would have looked at me calmly as though you knew all this already, even though I hadn't told you.

The hospital nurses were wonderful at teaching me how to breastfeed, how to bathe your little slippery body and trickiest of all, how to stick long safety pins through several layers of folded fabric nappies without pricking your skin.

On his next visit your dad told me that Tricia had offered to pass on to us lots of nappies and pins. A neighbour had lent us a carrycot, with sheets and blankets, to take you home.

I felt that we were being loved and cared for, with every need being met. This time by strangers.

The next day, I woke early. Ten days prior your dad and I had arrived at the labour ward of this hospital, unsure of our immediate future but caught up in the immediateness of a birth. Two of us had come, and now, thankfully, three of us would leave.

I would miss the nurses and their dedicated care, but I was excited by what was unfolding. Baby you, Garth, and I, along with a bag of clothes, bundled into the Beetle and set off for Wigginton. A new family filled the car. How would it be with all three of us in the caravan? When will the wedding be, I wondered?

Turning to look at me, your dad said, with a gentle smile, 'The wedding is tomorrow.'

18

A Family

I kept putting off telling you about your beginnings, Robbie, never imagining that we would not one day sit down face-to-face as adults. I suppose my reluctance in sharing how you came about was because I was sensitive to your opinion. I was waiting until you were older. But now, I can't tell you enough about how special you were right from the start, defying the odds against our being together. I think you wouldn't have cared one iota about the circumstances surrounding your birth, but I can only assume that.

Now, I face the prospect of being judged all over again. But, your overwhelmingly inspiring presence is here, loved and loving. Your energy is so positive that it overpowers my negative thoughts.

* * *

You, your dad and I settled contentedly into the caravan on that first night out of the hospital. It felt wonderful to have you there with us. As I nestled blissfully into Garth's arms I said quietly, 'It would be good if we could tell everyone the baby's name when they ask us tomorrow. Samuel is my favourite boy's name.'

'What about Edward? Rex and I both have Edward as a middle name,' said Garth.

'Not Edward, how about William?' I said. 'It's been in our family for generations.'

Then finally we agreed, not only on one name but three.

Tricia's neighbour Marina and her two young daughters, Josie and Susanne, had excitedly offered to look after you when we went to the ceremony.

'His name is Robert William Edward,' Garth told them, putting you, baby Robert, sleeping in your cot, on their living room floor. They nodded approvingly.

I felt guilty leaving you so soon, but we couldn't help it. Garth and I headed off to the Registry Office in Berkhamsted with Tricia and Chris.

Helen and John Stewart, and Jean, their daughter, all to be witnesses at our marriage, met us there. They smiled at us and Helen handed me a bouquet of orchids and lilies. I thanked her and announced your name to them all. John too nodded approvingly.

The celebrant shook hands with each of us. It was a brief ceremony and Garth and I said, 'I do'. We kissed. I looked at the others who were all beaming back at us.

After the signing we headed for the pub up the road. It had an old-world charm with a roaring open wood fire, timber bar, timber tables and chairs, leadlight windows and the smell of delicious food.

'Drink Guinness,' Helen told me. 'It's good for your milk production.'

So a large mug of dark froth-topped Guinness was put in front of me. I hadn't drunk alcohol for about a year, and even before that, only rarely, so I felt merry immediately, delighted to be amongst friends who all agreed that this was the happiest of outcomes for the baby, Garth and me.

Chris made a speech, and so did John, who told some jokes and laughing, we raised our glasses for yet another toast. Your dad thanked everyone for coming. We ate a hearty traditional roast lunch followed by a very English pudding, spotted dick with custard.

When we stepped outside we found the village market in full swing. John, walking next to me, said, 'I want to buy you something to mark this occasion.

Choose anything.' After scanning a stall full of nick-nacks, I chose a small hand-painted plate with a scene of two children under a tree picking apples. It had a scalloped pink edging and looked very English. It was to be the pretty little plate that I would hang on a wall in every house we lived in. You would have noticed it without knowing its significance.

It felt strange to have left you behind with relative strangers, so I scooped you up with joy on our return.

'He's been no trouble,' Marina and the girls chorused. 'He didn't cry. He slept nearly the whole time. We'll look after him whenever you need to go somewhere without him.'

There is a photo in the family album, taken on that day in the Newmans' garden after our return from the "wedding feast". It is of your dad in his Harris Tweed jacket holding you in his arms and gazing at you proudly. When you saw this photo, you would not have known how special that day was for many people.

That afternoon, Tricia and Chris invited the Stewarts back to Arbour House to meet you. Everyone smiled as we sat around you in the lounge room oohing and ahhing, delighted with this outcome. The months of dreading the future had culminated in the happiest day of my life. Now, I thought blissfully, I would have you and your dad in my life forever.

I hadn't fed you at night in the hospital so at first it was a novelty, even though you woke up every few hours. The three of us would snuggle up together while you suckled and then dozed. In the daytime, I fed you, changed your nappy and made you comfortable.

One day passing by the caravan, your dad told me that he looked in the window and saw me holding you in my arms, gazing at you with what he described as "pure love". It's precious to me that he told me that.

TOL from the adoption agency called and again expressed her surprise at what she considered an unexpected turn of events. She asked if there was still a chance we would consider giving up the baby.

'Absolutely not,' I said, categorically.

She repeated that she had hoped not to disappoint the couple she'd lined up to adopt our baby. After a short conversation about our plans she left and we never saw her again.

19

Settling In

In one way I felt bad that your birth and me marrying your dad were a *'fait accompli'* before I told Grandma and Grandpa. But I wanted to give them news about a more certain future than the indecisions of the months earlier. I knew they'd be excited to hear about you. I wrote a detailed aerogramme. On the outside I printed OPEN AND READ TOGETHER so that any shock they felt could be immediately shared. I promised a photo would follow in the next post.

Garth had written to Alli and Rex while I was in the hospital telling them of his imminent fatherhood and marriage.

I wrote to Sue. I knew she'd be delighted to hear about our newly formed family and received her reply in which she happily agreed to be your godmother.

We put the carrycot on the single bed and fenced it in with a chair. During sunny days you slept in a pram, also borrowed, under a tree in the garden until one day I found Miffy, the Newmans' cat snuggled up with you. From then I sat next to the pram when outside as we'd heard of cats accidentally smothering babies.

Your dad made a bespoke wooden box to fit the new cot mattress we bought. It was like a bigger, sturdier, more substantial version of a modern-day carrycot, minus handles, and it could easily fit across the back seat of the car. You slept in this little box and mattress in the caravan too.

During your first months as we headed into winter, your dad trussed you up tightly in a white woollen blanket. It worried me how tightly. He thought you were more likely to wake during the night if your hands escaped and got cold.

When I fed you during the night it was in our bed. There was nowhere else that was warm. It was easy to put you between us to keep warm and sometimes your dad and I both fell asleep during the feed.

I tried to be quiet when I got up to get you in the dark but I usually managed to kick the small radiator, which made a terrible clatter.

Fortunately, for your first seven months you didn't need floor space for crawling. I took you to the market each week where you were popular with the farmers and other stallholders.

We drove out further into the countryside on Sundays, and we walked across fields and over stiles, you in a borrowed baby-carrier on your dad's back. We visited the few people we knew. Occasionally we drove to see Helen and John in Cobham. One Sunday your dad's old school friends, who were on holiday in England, visited us. Allie came to Tring and stayed at a local hotel for a few days, and a month later Rex visited. Often we read, especially once the weather got warmer. You slept and gurgled on a rug between us in the garden.

Like many construction jobs, the finish seemed to drag on. As the building work became more mundane, Garth enjoyed it less. and talked more and more about going to Australia. Each time he did my heart sank. I had hoped we would stay in England for a couple more years, partly because I liked being there and partly because back in Australia I'd be embarrassed if anyone asked about when I was married. England offered me the freedom to be myself among relative strangers. But I would do whatever Garth decided.

In the meantime we were going to Cornwall for our first family Christmas. We would be in a big house with the Stewarts who especially loved you.

20

Christmas in Cornwall

On 23 December 1972 we pulled into the driveway of the Stewarts' holiday house in Cornwall. Helen, John, Jean and John junior all came out to greet us.

In the corner of the living room was the most stunning Christmas tree I had ever seen. While I stared at the delicate glass decorations everyone else was more interested in you, Robbie, sitting under it among the colourfully wrapped presents. When I look at the photograph taken that day, a photo you would have seen in an early family album, I know that no gift could have been more beautiful and precious than you. John senior and John junior took it in turns to cuddle you. Helen called you "Littlie" and loved having you there. You endeared yourself to them by smiling, looking straight into their eyes and rarely crying.

The next morning at breakfast, Helen announced that we would all be celebrating Christmas at a lighthouse on the north Cornish coast as a special treat. Late the next morning, on your first Christmas Day, we drove twenty minutes through torrential rain to reach the lighthouse. When we stepped out of the car the storm had stopped, but we were nearly blown sideways by the wind. I pulled my cloak closer around you while Garth hurried inside with your cot.

Like most lighthouses, this one was painted white and stretched up, smooth and elegant, a curved cylinder, towards the sky. The surrounding buildings were also painted white. Everything inside was neat and spotless. Outside from the rugged cliffs, I saw rocks and a raging surf far below.

The lighthouse keeper Clive and his wife Betty greeted us warmly. Along with their two children they had lived at the lighthouse for three years. Betty had to get the children to and from school every day in the bleakest of weather. She invited us into the cosy living room. It was bright with a highly decorated tree and a dining table set with a white linen tablecloth, red candles, crystal glasses and bonbons.

'Would you like to see the light before lunch?' Clive asked.

I put you, asleep now in your cot, in a bedroom and then one after the other we followed Clive up the tight spiral stairs. The top step opened out into a workroom where hung a giant ball made up of intricately pieced-together crystals. Garth asked about the mechanics behind the movement of the prism, which Clive eagerly explained. Close up it was a beautiful object. This magnificent crystal ball moved around smoothly and rhythmically, sending its warning beams out across the water. Through howling gales and bleak winters, reflections from all the crystal faces warned nearby ships of the treacherous rocks below. It made me think of Daphne du Maurier's novel *Jamaica Inn*, in which shipwrecks along this coastline were plundered of their cargo by locals, who often murdered the seamen. It was comforting to think of Clive, and all the lighthouse keepers before him, climbing the spiral staircase every day over the past 130 years, preventing death and disaster. I wondered if your Grandma's Cornish tin-mining ancestors had ever smuggled along this coastline.

Heading down to the dining room, I thought how appropriate this Christmas dinner was in contrast to the ones I experienced as a child.

At my Grandma's house in the central Victorian town of Inglewood, I remember Christmas was always hot. A forty-degrees dry heat did not stop your Grandma and your great-grandmother from cooking all day on woodfired hot plates and an oven to prepare a traditional English meal for about twenty people—brothers, aunts, uncles, cousins and friends. Your Grandma and my Grandma never complained as far as I knew, but it cannot have been much fun for them. As a child it was magical, a taste of an English-style Christmas in the stifling heat of an Australian summer. Grandma put threepences, sixpences and shillings into the English-style hot Christmas plum pudding. All of your Christmases after this one in Cornwall were spent with your dad, me, Jamie, Megan, Grandma, Grandpa and Kim and we still kept this English tradition.

At the lighthouse Betty had also worked hard to prepare a meal that couldn't have been more festive. As well as the turkey with chestnut stuffing, ham, roast potatoes and pumpkin, carrots, parsnips and Brussels sprouts, there was gravy, cranberry sauce and mustard. My mouth watered as Betty placed a plate of food in front of me. Just as I lifted my fork there was a cry from you from the bedroom. I stood up, but Helen said, 'Finish your meal, Margaret, he can wait a little longer.'

I felt a mother's urge to tend to you immediately but when Helen spoke, people did as she said. By the time I had put the last of the roast into my mouth, you were bawling and could no longer be ignored. I excused myself and hurried off to breastfeed out of sight. I could hear the merriment in the next room as everyone pulled bonbons and shared jokes and laughter.

Twenty-five minutes later when I rejoined the table, Betty carried in the large dome of a Christmas pudding followed by jugs of sweet white sauce and dishes of brandy butter. A delicious aroma arose from the bowls as Clive passed them around.

Robbie, I think of the photo taken at your last Christmas, Wahroonga, 1990. You are looking happy and content, lounging on the couch with your arm around Grandma, Jamie next to you. Grandma couldn't look more pleased to be there relaxing on Christmas Day with her two grandsons. Wrapping paper is strewn all over the floor. No-one felt the need to clean up immediately.

'We'll go to the beach tomorrow,' Helen announced later. 'There's a locked gate, but we have a key.'

I thought of Australia, the biggest continental island in the world with its extensive coastline and some of the most pristine beaches in the world, available to everyone. All you had to do was find a car park nearby. I had never imagined an exclusive beach with a locked gate.

Here on the north coast of Cornwall we welcomed a walk in the bracing wind along the fine yellow sand at Trevone Bay Beach after sitting and eating for hours the day before. No-one was swimming, though John said hardy swimmers did brave the water during winter, wearing wetsuits.

Sadly, the day came for us to leave the lighthouse, the beach, a large comfortable house and the Stewarts.

'This was the best family Christmas we could have had,' I said, hugging each of them.

Garth hugged Helen and Jean and thanked them too. He shook hands with the Johns. They all kissed you then your dad put you on the back seat of the Beetle, and we were off, back to our caravan at the bottom of the garden of Arbour House, Wigginton.

Garth was keen now to complete the conservatory. He was eager to start planning for our emigration as ten-pound poms to Australia.

21

Popular in Paris

Garth calculated a date that he could finish the conservatory. He organised your British passport, which shows your smooth six-month-old baby face, with a gentle smile looking straight at his camera. He also organised your registration as a white male South African citizen, written in Afrikaans and English.

With limited time left on this side of the world, I asked your dad if we could visit Paris. I went by train to London and enquired at several travel agents. One offered a package that included tickets for the ferry across the English Channel and the train from Calais to Paris, hotel accommodation and vouchers for meals in restaurants for either lunch or dinner.

Being in Paris in March 1973 invoked memories of my carefree days travelling with Sue and Chris in France. This time it was fun with responsibility. Madame Durant, the *maître d'* at the hotel, dressed in a black tailored suit over a coral pink blouse and wearing lipstick to match, welcomed us warmly and seeing you, stretched out her hands and asked if she could hold you. I nodded, and she scooped you up in her arms. You gazed up at her, and she laughed delightedly, touching your cheek.

We discovered that one of our meal vouchers was for an upmarket restaurant on the Champs-Élysées. We walked there and saw, through the large glass doors, starched white-linen tablecloths, silver cutlery, fresh flowers and gleaming glasses gracing all the tables.

A formally dressed, stern-faced waiter approached us, speaking in rapid French.

'Monsieur, Madame, bienvenue.'

We understood. I suddenly felt self-conscious, shabbily dressed in this elegant establishment and carrying a bundle of baby.

The smartly dressed supervisor joined us. She cooed over you and made us welcome. She held out a chair for me. I ordered beef bourguignon with steamed green vegetables and French fries. Garth was delighted when they offered to make him a vegetarian mushroom omelette with vegetables and a salad.

You lay on your blanket on the floor behind the table, staring with interest as the waiter, being careful not to step on you, served our delicious meal. We laughed and tried out our French on the waiter. All this while glimpsing the chic Parisian men and women outside, walking past the windows, all so trim and fashionably dressed, with carefully styled hair.

I had hoped that bringing you as a six-month-old baby to the sophisticated city of Paris wasn't too ambitious. We have a photograph of you, in a cold wintry scene at Versailles, bundled in a blanket and asleep on a stone bench. The bare branches of leafless trees are outstretched in the background of the photo, and I'm dressed in the red woollen cape Sue had lent me and long leather boots I had bought at a shoe sale.

You slept wherever you were laid down, often in public, and I fed you whenever needed. Passers-by admired you whether you were asleep or awake.

When we walked through the narrow streets of Montmartre, artists were drawing portraits. One young man wearing a black coat and beret was persuasive. He firstly drew then cut out a chubby-cheeked, button-nosed profile, which we thought did look like you. So we bought it. We kept it inside the cover of a family album. Perhaps you remember seeing it?

On a crowded Parisian train, an elderly lady stood up so that Garth could sit because he was carrying you. We warmed to French people. They were so kind to us, and we found them to have a genuine fondness for babies.

I carried you to the Louvre and headed towards the famous Mona Lisa. I paced backwards and forwards, intrigued, as her eyes followed me. Although there wasn't a crowd to peer over, some Japanese artists sitting some distance away were copying the famous face. I walked behind them to see their efforts, which were remarkable likenesses, but I couldn't tell if the eyes had the magic of the original.

While we were at the Louvre, Garth had gone to see if we could delay our return train trip by a day. We had organised to stay an extra night at the hotel so that we could go to a performance of the Folies Bergère. The maître d' had even agreed to babysit. Your dad found us in the gallery, still gazing at the Mona Lisa. He looked flustered. 'Hurry, we have to leave now.'

'But I haven't looked through the rest of the Louvre yet,' I protested.

'The train leaves in ninety minutes.'

'What do you mean?'

'The man at the station said the ticket date couldn't be changed.'

We ran back to the hotel, shoved all our gear into bags, breathlessly told the maître d' about the change of plan and raced off to the station, you jiggling in my tightly held arms. We rushed through the gates. The station attendant barely glanced at our tickets from a distance—any date could have been printed on them. There had obviously been some difficulty in translation between Garth and the station worker.

On our return home, the English people who asked us about our trip were surprised at how much we had enjoyed the French people and how friendly they had been.

'It must be because you're Australian,' they decided.

This time though, I knew that you were the X factor who had brought out the kindness and love in the French people and who had helped make our visit such a happy one.

22

A Melbourne Welcome

There was no room for all of your cloth nappies, baby clothes and cot blankets in the backpacks that Garth and I had always used up till now. 'We'll make canvas bags,' your clever dad said.

He drew a pattern on a large piece of paper, and we bought enough dark blue canvas, metal eyelets, thick thread and a long fat needle to make two bags. Garth handed me the neat pieces of material he'd cut out, then showed me where and how to sew them together. I would push the needle and thread through the thick cloth, regularly pricking my fingers.

After doing this every day for a couple of weeks we had two handsome bags. Your dad finished them off by sewing the metal eyelets along one side at the top and corresponding metal loops along the other side. The loops pushed through the eyelets, closing the flap, and a leather strap threaded through them. We added a padlock on the end for security, and wide canvas strap handles so that they were comfortable to carry. We used these bags for many years, so you would remember them.

On 26 April 1973, we left the caravan. Your dad and I took it in turns to carry either you or the luggage, and the Newmans drove us to Tring Station where, after a tearful farewell, we caught the train to Cobham to spend our last night in England with the Stewarts. More tears and then we caught a morning train to Heathrow, where we boarded a Qantas plane for the twenty-four-hour flight to Melbourne.

The flight attendants set up a cot for you at the front of the economy section with plenty of room for us to move around it. In the last two-plus years I hadn't missed the flat-vowelled Australian drawl but listening to the steward's voice, I felt immediately transported home. Hearing that old familiar twang made me excited and apprehensive.

Grandma and Grandpa had written saying how they had been shocked by my news initially, but how much they were looking forward to me coming home and meeting Garth and baby Robert. Grandma had longed for grandchildren and you were her first. She and Grandpa would be waiting for us at Melbourne Airport.

* * *

It was 28 April when we landed. Mum hugged me tightly, then said a warm hullo to Garth, who kissed her cheek. Then she stretched out her arms to you, who looked up and stared at her with interest. She looked at you adoringly. I realised that if there was any awkwardness among her friends, she would be sensitive to my feelings.

Grandpa, grinning, stretched out one large, rough, farmer-like hand, unlike most bank managers', and shook Garth's.

Your dad said he was happy to be in Australia, and yes we had had a good flight over. Grandma walked off, carrying you, while the rest of us took the luggage to the car.

Grandma and Grandpa could not be more pleased to see us, and I to see them, even though I still wished we were back in England. I was still worried that people would judge me critically if they found out about the dates of your birth and your dad's and my marriage.

We all lived together at Grandma and Grandpa's until after a few days they drove north to help look after Bill's farm. Your Uncle Kim, a teacher, shared the Melbourne house with us. It was a great help financially to have free accommodation but it was an adjustment to live in a home with another adult, for whom I also washed and cooked, and where there were polished antique furniture, crystal cabinets and ancient vases on display.

You were crawling now, opening cupboards and drawers and pulling out their contents, typical behaviour for a baby. I was worriedly aware of how Grandma had always kept the elegant interior polished and spotless.

You developed at an average rate in everything but speech. You said words early. One day I heard you talking to yourself. I looked in the dining room. You were fiddling with the key in the chiffonier. I listened carefully and heard, over and over, your rhythmically chanted words.

'Naughty boy, silly boy, a nuisance. Naughty boy, silly boy, a nuisance.' I could hear myself saying those words.

'Dear little Robbie,' I said, scooping you up and cuddling and kissing you. 'You are not a naughty boy, a silly boy or a nuisance. Mummy is silly to say that.'

I tried harder to put you before tidiness and housework. Grateful as I was for our rent-free accommodation, I looked forward to being in our own place.

Grandma and Grandpa gave us a substantial lump of money which they suggested could be part of a deposit on a house or to purchase a car. Your dad and I agreed that a car would give us the freedom we'd enjoyed with our Beetle in England. Also, until Garth had a job, we couldn't apply for a bank loan to buy a house. Garth chose a brand new Volkswagen station wagon.

'We could sleep in the back on a long trip,' he said. 'And the luggage goes in the front.'

We set off around Victoria in our Volkswagen, stopping in to see cousins and aunts and uncles and friends so that they could meet Garth and he could see a bit of Australia, and to show you off. I tried to change the subject if dates were mentioned and I felt uncomfortable, but mostly we were wholeheartedly welcomed.

You were healthy and happy, but on the advice of friends, I took you to the local baby health centre for a check-up. The prim childcare nurse, dressed in white, weighed and measured you.

'Average,' she pronounced, 'according to the statistics.'

'Do you want to have other children?' she asked.

Taken aback, I answered, 'Yes.'

'Well,' she said, 'you must stop breastfeeding. Your baby has had an excellent start, but nine months is long enough. Your body needs time to adjust for the next pregnancy.'

I was saddened to hear this, as you and I enjoyed breastfeeding both for the bond it had helped create between us and also because it was such an easy way to feed you. You were a contented baby, and it seemed unnecessary to stop as there was always plenty of milk. Regretfully, I weaned you to your distress and mine. The childcare nurse had sounded so authoritative. In England, without any peer comparisons, I would have followed my instinct.

A month after being back in Melbourne, Sue's sister Penny and I were matrons of honour at Sue's marriage to Gerald. Sue had a dressmaker sew a mid-length dark green velvet dress for each of us. The Windsor Hotel in Spring Street held the reception. Half the guests had come over from New Zealand, where Sue was going to live with Gerald on his family's cattle and sheep property on the South Island's Canterbury Plains. I had hoped Bert and Ben would attend the wedding, so Garth could reunite with old friends, but neither of them came.

In June 1973, with our financial responsibilities mounting, Garth wrote applications to umpteen construction companies. Even though he had graduated with a civil engineering degree from a South African university, he found it difficult to get a construction job, which was his preference, without any construction experience.

Finally, he got an offer for an interview with an Australian construction company. In the interview, he was asked why he had travelled around for years and not worked. Instead of this being seen as a negative, the interview panel saw Garth as an engineer who might be willing to move for new projects.

He started on the West Gate Bridge, which, only a few years before, had been the site of Australia's worst industrial accident. Thirty-five construction workers had died when a span of the bridge plummeted into the Yarra River mud. For Garth, I think, the job quickly lost its challenge. We were saving for a house now though, so his steady income was necessary.

* * *

A year later, your dad took two weeks off work and we headed up to Bill's farm for a holiday. The drive was two and a half days, but it was fun to be on the road again. Grandma and Grandpa, who were already there enjoying Queensland's warmth in winter, were excited to see us, especially you, walking and talking in short sentences.

You loved Grandma and Grandpa and us all being together. Your dad rode Bill's quietest horse, Nudge, with you sitting on the front. He held you tight, with you both sitting in the tray, when Bill steered the ute towards the big dam over bumps at the back of the property. You and your dad sat together in the shade of the brigalow trees and watched kangaroos sleeping. You yelled at the dogs if they jumped on you and kept an eye on Grandpa in the vegetable garden. You didn't whinge on the long drive back to Melbourne either, racing around on your plastic horse every time we stopped to stretch our legs, and seemed to enjoy the novelty of sleeping in motels.

A couple of months later, Grandma came back from Queensland to look after you while I returned to teaching three days a week. I missed you. The high school was a twenty-minute drive away, and my income was going to pay for things we would need in our new house, like a washing machine and a refrigerator. You spent the days happily with Grandma. She not only prepared delicious meals and snacks, but she also read to you and played games.

I taught for two and a half terms, but now I was over six months pregnant and stopped working. Grandma had a suggestion for when the birth was imminent. 'What if we take Robbie with us to the farm?' she asked 'Just to give you enough time to have the new baby? It'll only be for a couple of weeks.'

When the time came, Grandpa drove off slowly. Your serious face stared at me through the back window of the car. Was this the right decision? The only comfort was that it was just going to be two weeks. The house felt empty and quiet.

23

A Baby Brother

On 17 September 1974, your baby brother—Garth chose James, and I decided Llewellyn, but we called him Jamie—arrived deep-chested weighing nine and a half pounds, with dark hair in contrast to your blonde hair. He and I settled into a routine of breastfeeding and sleeping. Your dad and I wondered when you'd be back.

'How much longer, Mum?' I asked on the phone.' It's been a month since you went away.'

'We'll head back as soon as Bill returns from overseas. At most, two weeks from now.'

When you got out of the car after six weeks away, and a two-day drive, you stared and stared at me. For days afterwards, you followed me around like a shadow.

'I'm not going to leave you, Robbie,' I said, trying to reassure you.

You were two years old now, and we all often enjoyed the twenty-minute stroll to the shops in Glenhuntly Road, me pushing the pram and you holding onto it when we would cross a road. You would beam happily at everyone we passed and, looking up at them, say, 'Beautiful morning.'

'Yes,' most replied, smiling. 'It is a beautiful morning.' Then they would look into the pram and coo over Jamie. Many would say he was in a good paddock. The first time anyone said this, you looked puzzled. I explained what it meant.

I wonder if you would remember the time when, at the State Savings Bank of Victoria, we left the pram outside with Jamie fast asleep. Inside the bank, you hopped up onto a stool to draw on the deposit slips while I stood at the counter. Then you climbed up to sit on the shelf and chatted with the teller and showed her your drawing. We left, smiling.

At the butcher's, you drew circles and other shapes in the sawdust on the floor with your foot. The butcher, a jovial man who dressed in a blue and white striped apron, kept a jar of sweets on the counter, and he urged you to pick one. You looked at him, chose a black-and-white humbug and said, 'Thank you.' The butcher beamed.

'What lovely manners,' I heard a customer say.

We left the butcher's still smiling. Then we looked in the second-hand dealer's window at the old clocks and the silver and the cabinets. We left that shop smiling because of the funny large stuffed parrot we had spotted sitting on the back of an old chair.

We reached the corner—the last shop was the greengrocers. The greengrocer was a happy Greek man with a strong accent, always friendly and generous. We bought some vegetables, and, as I handed him the money I owed him, he said conversationally, 'No baby with you today?'

'Baby? Oh no!' I said, shocked. 'I left him outside the bank at least twenty minutes ago.'

I was not smiling when we hurried off, but found the pram still there and the baby still sleeping. Jamie hadn't noticed. How had both you and I completely forgotten that we had pushed the pram from home to the shops? How had we forgotten the baby?

'We'll have to be more careful, Robbie,' I said.

* * *

Jamie was three months old when we bought the double-brick house in

Bentleigh, a middle-class suburb with a busy shopping centre only a fifteen-minute stroll away. A routine of breastfeeding and sleeping for the baby meant we spent most days at home, apart from our daily walk to the Centre Road shops. You mostly played with your toys on the floor with Jamie on a rug next to you. You were his voice, and you seemed always to understand what he wanted when no-one else did. So began a very close relationship between you two.

You were a happy, bright, mostly obedient toddler but your tendency to wander caused your dad and me some anxious moments. Any house we had looked at to buy had to be child-safe as an essential feature. The Bentleigh house had a backyard enclosed by a high wooden gate that could be locked and a tall timber fence on three sides, perfect, we thought, to keep you in.

The first time I noticed the house unusually quiet, I found you chatting to our friendly American neighbour over the fence way up the back of our deep block. She was standing up on something behind the fence, looking over at you. I went up to chat too. She said she missed her grandchildren in the States, and how well you talked for your age—two years and four months.

The second time I missed you, I found you around the side of our house chatting to our neighbour on the left. You had thrown all your toys over the fence, and she had thrown them back. You enjoyed this interaction, so repeated it often.

The third time, when I couldn't find you anywhere in the yard, I noticed that the gate was ajar. Out on the street, I saw a tiny blonde-headed figure wearing a red jumper heading down towards the quiet intersection.

'Robbie!' I called, as calmly as I could. You turned around, saw me, and stopped, but when I started running towards you, you ran too. You turned around the corner and kept running, your little legs barrelling up a street that led to a road with heavy traffic. Trucks thundered along at speed, motorbikes roared past and cars honked. I ran faster and got close, but you thought this was a game, so you ran more quickly still, laughing. I was almost out of breath but with a last-ditch effort I lunged and grabbed you by the back of your jumper. As we walked home, back to baby Jamie, I gave you a stern lecture about wandering away from the house by yourself. Did you listen?

The answer to that question came on a weekend with my cousin Yvonne and her husband Ted at their farm near Swan Hill—where you as a teenager water skied—when we were packing the car to leave after a late lunch. As I strapped Jamie in the back seat, I called out.

'Come on, Robbie, we're leaving. Hop in the car.' We all expected you to appear immediately, but you didn't.

Looking around, Yvonne said, 'Where's the dog? Misty's not here.' Then, in a panicky voice, she said, 'I don't mean to alarm everyone, but a child fell into one of the open irrigation canals last year and drowned.'

Sick to the stomach now, I headed off to the nearest canal with Garth. We searched in opposite directions. The water was calm but deep and dark brown. The sides were too steep for a toddler to climb out. There were no barriers, and I shuddered at the thought of you falling in. Like most children, you loved playing with water. Ted headed off down the road while Yvonne stayed at the house with Jamie, hoping you were close.

'How far could his little legs take him?' Ted asked. But we didn't know how long ago you had left, except that no-one had seen you since lunch.

We got back to the house wondering where else to look and were on the verge of calling the police when the phone rang. It was a neighbour, a kilometre away.

'I'm not sure if it's your dog, Yvonne,' she said, 'but one that looks like Misty walked past here a while ago with a toddler. I thought you might like to know.' The knot in my stomach eased, and Garth's expression relaxed. We drove to pick you up, and when we found you, walking along the dusty country road with Yvonne's dog trotting along a few paces ahead of you, I asked, 'Were you lost, Robbie?'

'No,' you answered seriously, 'but the dog was lost.'

24

Life in The Suburbs

Our main social outings were company functions when wives were invited too, perhaps to an expensive restaurant or a resort out of town. A babysitter had to be found, which was fine when Grandma and Grandpa were not in Queensland, but difficult if they were. Betsy, my school friend and her husband, Chester, kindly cared for you on some of those occasions. I would have liked to meet up more often with old school friends, but with two little ones, it didn't happen very often. Friends occasionally came for lunch or dinner, or we would visit them. So as it turned out, you, and your baby brother, Jamie, were my main companions.

Sometimes, if Garth had Saturdays off, he would suggest that I have the car packed and ready to leave when he arrived home from work on Friday night. Then we could immediately drive the four and a half hours to our family's holiday shack at Wandiligong in the foothills of the Victorian Alps.

Stepping out of a warm car, shivering in the cold night air, I'd feel for the key to the gate in a eucalyptus hollow, breathing in the strong smell of the peppermint gums. On opening the door to the cottage, we would often disturb microbats that had taken up residence in the crevices between the walls and ceilings.

I'm not sure that you knew that Grandpa had trucked five huts from Mount Beauty in 1959. These former workmen's huts had been sold off after the

Kiewa Hydroelectric Scheme finished. He put them up on stumps and joined them with wide passages. Grandma had decorated them to create comfortable and cosy accommodation that could sleep eight. Of course you know how cosy she had made the rooms.

We loved those weekends in the peaceful surroundings of the tree-covered hills. I would drink the cup of tea that Garth brought me in bed, listening to the orchestra of the kookaburras, currawongs, magpies, king parrots and galahs. During winter, scarlet robins, red-capped robins and golden whistlers would flitter in and out of the grevilleas, down from the snow-covered mountains. Garth and I grubbed out blackberries, bracken and wattle. We'd stack them in a pile to burn in the late afternoon. You would help drag sticks over to the heap.

On hot evenings we sometimes drove to a public gas barbecue at the Ovens River in Bright where there was a playground for you with a swing to ride on and slides to whizz down. We cooled off in the river, you under Garth's arm as he swam across to the opposite bank. I'd paddle with Jamie on the edge.

Some mornings, we'd walk straight up the valley from our block and spot kangaroos and wallabies. If we saw an echidna or lizard up close, Garth would point out its details to you. We'd return to Bentleigh, but wished we could stay at Wandi longer.

* * *

After two years in Melbourne, the construction company offered Garth a promotion to build a civic centre in Townsville. I was not at all sure about going with him immediately because I was seven months pregnant with our third child. Grandma made a suggestion.

'You have a good obstetrician here, booked into the hospital and you have two toddlers. Why don't you let Garth find somewhere to live in Townsville? You have the baby in Melbourne, and then join him?'

I put this idea to your dad.

'No,' he said. 'I want you all to come with me.'
So, we all went together.

25

Townsville and a Baby Sister

In mid-April 1976 the hot wind and ninety percent humidity hit us on the tarmac at the Townsville airport. I wonder if you'd remember how hot it was when we stepped off the plane from Melbourne?

We caught a taxi to our motel on the other side of town where the air conditioning gave us some relief. But our room soon became a prison.

Your dad would leave for work early and usually be home for dinner in the motel restaurant. He was away for more than twelve hours. You, Robbie, saved me from losing my mind because you entertained Jamie non-stop. You invented all sorts of games with matchbox cars and building blocks. You'd hide in cupboards and throw soft toys around. You'd do drawings for hours with Jamie beside you, copying. In the afternoons, we read books and then we all had a nap.

Our motel was a couple of kilometres out of town, so there was nowhere to walk out of the heat, and our car was still on a train coming up from Melbourne.

It was three weeks before the agent looking for a company rental for us found one. We moved into a white-painted brick house with a pink bougainvillea growing along the front wall and a fenced yard at the back. Inside, our eyes had to adjust to the bright blue carpet that spread everywhere but the kitchen. 'It'll show every speck of dirt,' I said to no-one in particular.

Within a week, you and Jamie discovered a pipe sticking out from a wall at the back of the house. You stuck the hose in it and turned on the tap. We came home from shopping to discover the blue carpet dark and spongy underfoot. Garth and I pulled up the carpet and hired industrial fans to dry out the concrete slab before stretching the carpet back to the edges as best we could, all of which made it an even brighter blue.

It was on 10 June 1976, that your sister Megan Elizabeth was born after a dramatic last-minute dash to Townsville Base Hospital, which was constructed in levels on the side of Castle Hill. First, every one of the traffic lights turned red. Then Garth, panicking because I was having difficulty trying to stand up in the passenger seat of the Volkswagen and moaning that I could feel the baby's head coming out, parked two levels too low in the car park.

A matron conducting an antenatal class saw me waddling and commandeered a workman to help Garth carry me to the lift. Unfortunately, the elevator was out-of-order, so they continued up two flights of stairs.

As soon as I lay on the bed, a nurse whipped off my clothes, and your baby sister emerged with only pressure marks across her forehead as evidence of the last-minute rush to the hospital.

Your dad brought you and Jamie to visit her. You looked at her sleeping contentedly and wondered why she didn't have any hair. Mostly you and Jamie wanted to tell me what you were doing with Grandma and Grandpa, who had driven up from Melbourne to look after you both.

When I left Townsville Base Hospital, we were now a family with three little ones under four. I couldn't have managed at the start without Grandma and Grandpa's help. The day they left I felt desperate, wondering how I would cope.

You'd probably have a memory of being admitted to the same hospital a month later for a hernia operation. It was a small protrusion out of your belly button, not dangerous, but the doctor thought it was better to repair it early. I left you in the children's ward that night, sitting on top of the big bed. You looked so small and serious. The next afternoon, after your operation, I found you in the nursery playing Lego with the other kids. You looked pleased to see me but were not desperate to leave. Other children, who had to stay longer, looked at you enviously when we left.

Garth needed the car to get to work, but I needed it once a week to go shopping. On those days, we'd all have to be dressed before six to drop him off at the construction site. One morning we returned home with our groceries to find that the house had flooded again. How? A plug had been left in a basin, and a leaky tap dripped into it. The carpet was again dark blue and squelchy underfoot, and for a second time, Garth and I pulled it up.

This time, rather than hiring powerful commercial fans, we spread the carpet out along the fence to dry in the wind. It didn't fade, was clean, and was bluer than ever.

Coincidentally, the owner arrived that day to introduce himself. Fortunately he hadn't asked to look around so after a brief chat on the front doorstep, I shut the door, relieved that he hadn't spotted his carpets swinging in the breeze along the back fence.

Across the road from our house was a vast, desolate, treeless expanse of dry grass designated to be a football ground. Empty blocks surrounded us except for the one house next door where Trevor lived with his family.

Trevor was about your age, four and a half, with brown rotting teeth. He'd wander into our kitchen some days carrying a bowl of rice bubbles covered in white sugar and no milk. After about ten minutes I'd ask him to leave. He smelt so bad. I gently asked him one day if he ever had a bath. He looked at me as though I was mad and muttered, 'Crabs.'

One day he persuaded you and Jamie to go into their house, and you came home with the news that their bath was full of live mud crabs. Neither of you ever wanted to go there again. Their house smelled terrible. The reason for Trevor's smelliness was solved, and I realised that at least some of his diet was gourmet.

One morning you ran in yelling, 'Trevor's brothers shot me.' Sure enough, there was an angry red mark on your leg. Jamie, who was two and a half years old at the time and ever-loyal and ready in your defence, shouted, 'Where are they Rob? I'll get 'em,' and ran outside. I went out after him and learnt that it was a fishhook fired from a Shanghai air rifle and told the twelve-year-old twins never to shoot over the fence again.

Your dad, in the meantime, was supervising the building of the civic centre, which was to be used for concerts and theatrical performances. He left at six every day but Sunday and arrived home never before seven in the evening.

I was fortunate that Megan was a happy, easygoing, undemanding baby. Friends in Melbourne had sent me lovely, mostly pink dresses for her in which she looked beautiful. Yet because her hair was slow to grow, people still asked if she was a boy.

We knew no-one in Townsville and the construction company didn't offer much in the way of social activities. Once again, I was so fortunate that you made up games and entertained Jamie, who always contributed loudly with brrrms and eeh aah eehaahs. You also included Megan, when she was old enough. I was thankful that here, in this place, you didn't wander. When you made up stories with characters, played by you and Jamie, you gave Megan the character neither you nor Jamie wanted, but she was just glad to be included.

Although Saturdays when Garth didn't work were rare, on those free weekends he was keen to go camping, but he knew I wouldn't go again without a proper bed to sleep on. So, after work at nights he made a bespoke trailer for two mattresses. His workmanship on anything he made was perfect in every detail. I heard later that his father, Rex, also a skilled craftsman, had modified a yacht in his spare time, and enjoyed sailing it with friends in Natal.

* * *

A year later Townsville improved for me when we moved into a charming old Queenslander on Castle Hill. This house was on stilts with wide verandahs, large rooms, and louvre windows that let in any cool breeze. It also came with friendly neighbours.

I started a postgraduate course in special education at James Cook

University. A sweet babysitter, tall with a blonde ponytail, came several times a week. She was studying at the university to be a teacher, and you and the others enjoyed being with her.

I settled into a more productive, varied and rewarding lifestyle. Then one day Garth came home and said we were moving to Dysart.

'Where on earth is Dysart?' I asked.

'It's about a six-hour drive away in the Bowen Basin, central Queensland.'

I tried to take this in.

'We're going to live in a donga,' he added. He seemed to think that I'd be pleased.

'Live in a what?' I said.

I told you what your dad had told me, that we were moving to inland Queensland and that our house, a donga, would come on the back of a truck and be put down in a paddock. I found it hard to imagine. I wonder if you did too?

26

Life in Bulldust

Grandma told her friends that we lived like gypsies. She never got used to the peripatetic nature of our life as a construction engineer's family. Some engineers we knew either worked and lived in only one town or else they moved to the job alone while their family stayed at home, and their children attended one school. But Garth liked the variety in projects, which meant shifting around to different places, and he always wanted us to move with him as a family. There was no exception.

We drove the six hundred kilometres from Townsville in north Queensland to Dysart, a town established four years earlier as a service town for nearby coal mines. It had at its centre one bank, one supermarket and one pub motel, the Jolly Collier, the only place to stay.

After dumping our stuff inside, we drove to look at Garth's work site where we would also soon be living. About two kilometres out of town, he pulled up and said, 'Here it is.' I looked at the acres of an almost-bare, flat paddock next to the road.

'There's the office,' he said, pointing to a shed-like building, 'and there's the donga the other two engineers will be living in.'

'Where's ours?' I asked.

'Ours is a bigger brand-new one. It'll be arriving soon and will be put near these buildings, so the three dongas will be in a cluster fifty metres apart. Can you see some caravans up beyond that group of gums? That's where all the workers with families live and over beyond the caravans, but to the left, is where the single men live.'

You and I could just make out the caravans in the distance, but could not see the single men's quarters.

I had known that this new experience would begin in a motel, as it had in Townsville, without housework or cooking, but those advantages soon paled in the confined space with the whole family itching to spread out.

One morning, after we had been in the Jolly Collier for a couple of weeks, Garth asked if we wanted to see our donga being unloaded.

We stood in the eight-acre paddock near the patch of ground allocated for our dwelling and watched wide-eyed as a massive semitrailer lumbered up the flat dirt track, with our house on top. I could see it was longer than the other two dongas but made of the same dusty white cladding. The truck stopped, lowered its load, and then plonked it unceremoniously on the ground. With the bang, a huge pall of black dust rose, then settled down again. I'd never seen bulldust before, but with a talcum powder consistency it covered everything it touched.

The donga's only door was in the centre of the wall, with a high step up. Once inside, I walked left into an area about eight metres by six metres. Along one wall were cupboards. The kitchen's workbench, oven, cooktop and refrigerator were taped, so they had stayed in place during the move. A timber table and six chairs stood taped onto the timber-look floor. The adjacent room had a double bed and a tiny ensuite. Down a passage was a toilet, then a laundry with a washing machine and trough, a shower, and washbasin. The next two rooms were small bedrooms with two single beds in one, and a single bed in the other.

I don't remember if you chose a bedroom, or if you let the others choose. I do know that both Jamie and Megan would have wanted to share a room with you.

Everything was brand new, which I appreciated. The feature I came to appreciate more than anything was the two air conditioners which ran 24/7. They made living in a box with no insulation, plonked in the middle of a bare paddock, bearable.

Garth was the civil engineer in charge of designing and erecting seven bridges over a railway line to connect Dysart to Moranbah, the site of several massive open-cut coal mines which were the primary source of employment in the Bowen Basin. The bridges made access across the railway line possible for farmers and other residents in the area.

The other two engineers, John and Michael, who shared a donga, had different roles. Michael was in charge of the earthworks along the line, and John was in charge of the project overall. John explained that his wife had elected to stay with their two sons in Townsville. She didn't fancy living in a dusty paddock, and her sons were at a school they liked. So John flew home every second weekend. Michael was a bachelor with a private plane which he flew on weekends.

The sight of large equipment and machinery taking up the entire width of the two-lane road, and more, never ceased to startle us.

Because you were five now, I felt that you'd better attend the school in Dysart, so I took you along on the first day of term two. I met the nervous young teacher who looked warily around at the rowdy youngsters in her classroom, all yelling and fighting. Poor thing, I thought. She was straight out of teachers college. I had misgivings about how much teaching she would do.

'What did you learn at school?' I asked when I picked you up.

'Nothing.'

'What did you do at lunchtime?'

'A boy chased me trying to bite me so I stayed on top of the slide in the playground. A gang of boys was waiting at the bottom, yelling at me.'

'Do you want to go back tomorrow?'

'No,' you said.

Of course, I didn't send you back. At the small Dysart shopping centre, you used to look intently at the trolley wheels when mothers of school-age children stopped and asked,

'How old is he?'

'Five,' I would reply.

'What's wrong with him?' they would ask in condescending voices.

'There's nothing wrong with him,' I would say, moving away.

'Well, why isn't he at school?'

'I must finish the shopping,' I'd reply, walking off and thinking, that school is totally inadequate and probably doing their children harm. Teaching you at home was a much better option.

So each morning, after Garth had walked across to the office donga and we had finished breakfast, and I'd cleared away the dishes, you and I sat at the table. You'd look at the simple arithmetic puzzles I'd written out for you on a piece of paper and quickly write down the correct answers, rarely asking questions.

Jamie and Megan would spread out on the floor with their large sheets of paper. Jamie would start drawing a big colourful picture with pencils, and Megan would try to copy it. When you drew pictures, Jamie would try to copy yours.

We read stories, and I asked you questions about them. You wrote sentences and read books to yourself.

The office donga, about a hundred metres away, was close enough for Garth to come home for a quick lunch. 'What have you little tykes been up to?' he would ask, and you three children would eagerly present a drawing or some writing or tell him a story.

After lunch, when your dad had returned to work, we would all lie down together on the double bed and read three books, one chosen by each of you.

When I told my mother, a qualified and experienced primary school teacher, about all of this, she disapproved.

'He learns so quickly,' I told her, 'I only have to show him something once, and he can repeat it, whatever the subject. Just ask Rob what his one day at Dysart Primary School was like.'

Fortunately, your dad supported me in my decision about your schooling.

Miles, a boy of your age, did go to school and lived with his mother Maureen and his father Steve up in the construction camp's caravan park, about half a kilometre from our donga. Steve was a carpenter and supervisor, so he assumed a prime location in the park as positions for caravans were determined by rank in the job. After Steve suggested it to Garth, you sometimes went up to Miles' caravan in the afternoon when he had come home from school. After the first visit, I asked what you did.

'I read,' you said.

'Has Miles got many books?'

'No, he doesn't have any books, he's got comics.' You'd never seen comics before and loved them, but I never did buy any.

'Miles' place has a fence and a garden and a path from their gate to their door,' you said. I thought this was extraordinary for a caravan, so I went up to see for myself and to ask Maureen how it got there. As it turned out, every caravan had a concrete path to its door, and many had a fence and garden.

'Yes,' Maureen said, 'we all make a home the minute we arrive at a new job. We travel all around Australia, and so we have to make the most of wherever we end up working. Steve and some other men make the paths a priority. We want to keep the dirt out. I do the garden. We have to do something in these isolated places. There's no work for us women.'

I asked Garth if we could have a paved path to the door to help alleviate bulldust coming into the donga. It wasn't a top priority for him.

'Remember you have a house,' he said, 'they don't.'

Not long before we left, a path was laid to our donga.

Most days, before the temperature rose to unbearable levels, you kids played in the bulldust. That fine black powder ingrained itself everywhere, despite me putting a bucket of water at the door to dip your hands and feet into before you all came back inside.

You would play games, often with matchbox cars and Star Wars figures, "starwies", you called them. You'd invent stories and allocate different characters amongst yourselves and have a running dialogue. Jamie provided elaborate sound effects. Megan was included by being told what to say and do.

Sometimes you played in the massive shed where Garth kept our trailer, the one he had made by hand and where the company's earthmoving equipment was stored.

One afternoon, Jamie and Megan came screaming back to the donga. 'Wasps have bitten Rob,' they said. I rushed out to find your face red and puffy, your eyes swollen closed and you, who never cried, holding back tears.

You and Jamie had been playing in the shed under the trucks. Usually, Garth was there but not this time. You had put your head under a machine into a nest of wasps. They had bitten you all over. You sat quietly sobbing while I dabbed at the swollen mass with cold water and put you to bed where you fell asleep. You endured the pain of those bites with little fuss and within a week, the swelling had subsided.

The single men's quarters were about half a kilometre from us, across the paddock in a different direction from the caravans. Tony, a young, newly graduated engineer, lived there. He walked past our donga on his way to the office.

'Tony is always singing and eating an apple,' you told me. Tony liked you three children. He was lonely at the camp and missed his younger siblings.

When he passed by, you joked with him and he offered to babysit if I wanted to play golf at the local course which started with six holes and ended with nine during our time there. The government was suggesting a change to the remote area tax allowance. In protest, workers in the surrounding mines went on strike. Many of the men spent their days creating another fairway and gravel-green. Having Tony babysit you was a happy arrangement for us all.

Weekends away were the favourite part of our time at Dysart. Outside a family-friendly motel consisting of units along the beach, at Bucasia, a beach north of Mackay, the sand was white, and the sea bright aqua and inviting. Here, you were all free to run in and out of the cabin, finding shells, dead fish and seaweed.

At the first visit, you ran inside, yelling excitedly about seeing hundreds of blue crabs. Garth and I looked to see a platoon of soldier crabs outside, all marching along the damp firm sand, purposeful and spectacular. A spotter crab was keeping guard at each entrance hole, ready to raise the alarm.

Your eagle eyes, Robbie, found things that the rest of us didn't notice. On the beach, you found unusual shells and colourful rocks, coins, keys, and other flotsam and jetsam washed in on the tide.

The sea was sparkling, and the waves lapped gently close to shore. So we all swam in the shallows. But Garth went out further. Your dad seemed fearless in swimming far out beyond the breakers.

At low tide, we could walk across a sandbar, about a kilometre across, to another beach, which was called Sunset Bay. We needed to be careful to watch the tide to avoid being trapped on the wrong side. You were tall enough to walk through the water up to your chest when the tide was coming in. Garth would put Jamie on his back and Megan on mine.

During our last few months at Dysart, we planned our first overseas trip together to the land of your father's birth, South Africa. Megan had lots of lovely clothes to wear handed on from my school friends, who had girls, but you and Jamie didn't have any.

'Why don't I cut out patterns, and you could sew them?' Garth suggested. We were doing everything we could to save money for travelling so making rather than buying clothes sounded like a great idea.

'Stand still,' said Garth, holding the measuring tape across your shoulders. 'Stop giggling,' he said, as he stretched the tape around Jamie's chest and under his arms. He took leg measurements for shorts then drew them on a sheet of brown paper and cut them out. The next weekend away, we shopped in Mackay for the material. Garth's exact measurements and drawings meant the brown and blue shorts and white checked shirts fitted perfectly. You boys looked smart in your new outfits. Garth designed a skirt for me too, which I also sewed.

My efforts to grow our vegetables were less successful. Turnips grew, but it took a lot of ingenuity to present them appetising as well as much stoicism from the family to eat them. A huge watermelon was my pride and joy which I showed at a Friday night barbecue.

'Where did you grow it?' one of the men asked suspiciously. I explained that I had chosen a patch of moisture to plant seeds far from our donga simply because of its permanent dampness. No-one ate it once they discovered it had grown in the single men's quarters' septic outflow. Of course, the site wouldn't have affected the fruit, but the perception it created did.

At the last Friday night barbecue, Garth and Steve organised a Sunday trip in our canoe.

We all went to the starting point. 'Why aren't you wearing a shirt?' I asked Miles.

'We're not going to be out for long,' he said. We watched as he and his dad, sitting upright in the canoe, vanished around a bend in the fast-flowing river. We drove straight to the meeting spot, but the canoe hadn't arrived. We waited until we were too hungry not to eat the picnic but saved some for them. We muttered about them being so long and lay down on a rug and had a nap.

'When is Miles getting here?' you asked, puzzled. We were all puzzled. Where on earth are they?

At dusk, we drove back to the camp to see if somehow they'd returned there. Garth and I drove in the dark to various parts of the river, the headlights picking up spiders and webs as big as dinner plates. Maureen was distraught. Michael gave her a bottle of brandy to help her get through the night of anxious waiting. She kept trying the walkie-talkie connected to Steve's truck in an increasingly slurred voice.

The next morning, Michael, in his two-seater plane with Garth as a spotter in the passenger seat, flew low along the river, but there was no sign of man or boy or canoe.

It was late morning when I saw Steve walking towards the camp. Apart from being sunburnt, blistered, thirsty, hungry and tired, he was fine. What had gone wrong? What we saw as a fast-flowing river when they started had petered out, and they had had to walk, carrying the heavy canoe along the meandering dry riverbed. When night fell, they took shelter under a tree only to get hammered by mosquitoes. They saw and heard the plane go over but couldn't get out into the open fast enough.

'I got pretty hungry,' said Miles, 'but Mum says I don't have to go to school tomorrow so that my sunburn and blisters can get better.'

The job was almost finished and packing up the site well underway when everyone on-site met at the very last barbecue, this one on a Wednesday night before people started leaving the camp. The main topic of conversation between everyone was around the questions, 'Where are you going next?' and 'What is your next job?' Many of the men, whether single or with a family, moved to the next construction as a group.

'What's your dad's next job? Where are you heading?' Miles asked you.

'South Africa. Dad's got five weeks off work,' you said.

'Might you be mauled by a lion?'

'Hope not, nor attacked by a hippopotamus. Dad says they're really dangerous.'

27

South Africa

It was during part of October, November and December 1978 when we were in South Africa. Do you remember the first people we met there? You pointed out those groups of children, not much older than you, waving excitedly at our hire car as we drove to the Kruger Game Reserve. 'What are they doing?' you had asked.

'Selling stuff,' said Garth. 'Let's see.'

We stopped and stared through the windows at the eager grinning faces.

'How old are you?' I asked one little boy closest to my side of the car.

'I am eight years old,' he answered and held up a carving of an elephant for us to see. 'I make it. See, tusks, trunk, ears.'

The boy behind him thrust forward a carved zebra. 'I make this one. This one beautiful zebra,' he said, smiling, showing a row of pearly white teeth.

'Buy mine, buy mine, cheap, mine cheap,' others chorused, holding up their pieces.

'The elephant is good,' you said quietly.

'The birds are too,' said Megan.

'I like the lion,' said Jamie.

We felt guilty about disappointing both groups of children, but this was only the first day of our trip and we didn't want any extra luggage just yet.

Before arriving at the game reserve, we had been travelling for days. Rivers had flooded overnight making it a stressful eight-hour detoured drive from Dysart to Bill's farm to leave our car and trailer. During that anxious drive you had plenty of opportunities to yell out "floodway" when you read the sign. From Bill's we piled into a bus to Brisbane, which took five hours, then, after a three-hour wait at the airport we flew to Sydney. From Sydney the flight to Perth took four hours. From Perth we had the twenty-hour flight to Johannesburg.

It was no wonder you children and I were all so tired by the time we arrived at Pretoriuskop Camp. It reminded me of the bus journey across Europe Garth and I had made all those years ago before you were born, except that now we had a family in tow. But just like then travelling seemed to energise your dad. Plus, after a decade of being away, he was excited to be back in his homeland.

'I'm setting the alarm for an early start tomorrow,' he announced. 'We must be out of the camp gates as soon as they open before sunrise, if we are going to see the game.'

The excitement in his voice was infectious. I fell asleep dreaming of herds of elephants. The next morning we drove around for half an hour in the cold and dark and saw nothing. I wished I was back in bed. You commented that it might be too early for the animals to be up yet and then suddenly someone—was it you?—pointed at a bush with two big brown eyes shining through it.

'It's a kudu,' said Garth, and then we all saw the long bony face those eyes belonged to. As we gradually adjusted to the stillness, shape and colour of the vegetation, the slightest movement alerted us to yet another animal.

'There's a deer,' you cried.

'There's another one,' said Jamie.

'I can see one too,' said Megan.

Sure enough, a herd of delicate, light-footed impalas sprang into view. 'They will run about eighty kilometres an hour if a lion is chasing them,' Garth said.

Back at camp, we met a disappointed couple. They had cruised around the reserve for several hours but sighted no game. They must have started too late, we muttered to ourselves smugly. Also, your dad was a knowledgeable guide.

Later in the morning as the temperature rose, we wandered down to the camp's natural swimming pool. We discovered that a family of baboons had got there first. Young ones were wrestling while bigger ones lazed on the rocks. On seeing us coming, a native boy, the pool's caretaker, started yelling and whistling and throwing stones at the animals. 'They could get aggressive,' Garth said, as the baboons reluctantly retreated to the trees along the edge.

We jumped in and swam in the clear, fresh cold water. Swimming in still water was dangerous in Africa because of the risk of contracting bilharzia or snail fever. Your dad said this pool fed by a fast-moving stream was safe.

That evening while cruising around, your dad suddenly stopped the car.

'Wow,' he whispered. 'Look at that. A fresh kill.'

Through the windows, we saw a lioness with two cubs ripping and tearing into a fresh zebra carcass on the road in front of us. The animals ignored us so we stayed and watched, mesmerised.

'How did they catch the zebra?' you asked.

'It would have been slower and weaker, and the lioness would have separated it from the herd,' your dad said.

'Poor zebra,' Jamie said.

'Yes,' Megan added, looking sad.

'It's the way the animals survive,' said Garth. 'They only kill what they need to feed themselves and their family. Look over there.' A hyena, on the side of the road, was waiting its turn. 'And up there,' he said, pointing. We watched a flock of vultures circling overhead, ready to feast on the pickings.

It took everyone else a few minutes to spot the first giraffe after I'd caught a slight movement behind some fever trees. Despite its dramatic height, shape and colouring it was camouflaged until it moved.

With practice we all got better at spotting game, especially when Garth added the incentive of giving five cents to whoever first saw an animal that day.

On the third day, desperate to keep up with her brothers Megan yelled out that she'd seen something. Sceptical, we all chorused, 'Where?'

At precisely that moment, an elegant impala appeared from behind a bush and stepped across the road. 'There,' Megan yelled, surprised and delighted.

Of all the animals in Africa, rogue elephants were amongst the most dangerous, Garth had said. Do you remember how terrified we all were when that lone elephant suddenly appeared and came running towards our car, trumpeting angrily, ears flaring? Fortunately, it veered off the road into the bushes before hitting us.

Warthogs were endearing with their comical faces, running around the camp with their tails pointing straight up in the air like aerials. Then there were meerkats standing up on their hind legs as if on lookout duty.

After a magical week on safari, we drove four hours north to Natal to meet your South African grandparents.

It had been more than six years since Garth and I had seen his parents, Allie and Rex, in England when you were a few months old, Robbie. The closer we got to the farm the more excited you kids became, but when we drove up their long drive past green paddocks dotted with black Angus cattle, you all became quiet and shy.

Allie and Rex came out to the car. They looked the same as they had in England and greeted us formally. We adults hugged each other while you children looked on. They said hello to each of you.

'What would you like the children to call you?' I asked.

They looked at each other before Allie answered, 'Allie and Rex.'

You all looked a bit surprised about being told to call grandparents by their first names.

Allie was eager to sort out where you children would be sleeping. She had borrowed a caravan that could fit two of you. There was a third bed in Rex's dressing room, she explained. Your dad and I looked at each other. Separating you three would be tricky.

Megan, who was not yet three years old, decided it by stating firmly, 'I want to sleep where Rob sleeps.'

So that meant you two would be in the caravan. Jamie wanted to join you, but then Rex said Jamie could choose a pipe from the rack over the bed where there was, we discovered, a grand selection of smoking pipes in all sorts of colours and shapes and sizes.

Garth said that in the past Rex always had a pipe in his mouth. Now Rex told Garth he had given up smoking since his recent cancer scare.

Allie announced that she had prepared steak for dinner.

'Oh, Mum,' said Garth, 'I don't eat meat anymore. I'm a vegetarian.'

'What?' she said, clearly annoyed, 'How long has that been going on?' Then she hurried off to tell the cook to prepare something else for Garth.

* * *

Rex hired Alfred to do the farm work, like moving the cattle and erecting fencing. Like many blacks (that is the term I was told they preferred), he was paid mainly with meat. Rex also gave him a plot to grow vegetables for his family and a field for a cow.

Alfred had eight children. One morning three of them—two were about the same ages as you, Megan and Jamie—came up to the caravan. Together on the front lawn you tossed a ball and tried talking to each other. You did your underarm squeaking trick. Jamie did his underarm trick too. Megan's trick was squeaking her ear. The three black children, two boys and a girl, stared at these unique displays by three white children. Then Allison, a boy named after Garth's mother, asked you if he could feel your blonde hair. You all shared the same curiosity. All three of you reached out to touch their black, oily spring coils and they felt your soft, straight, fair hair.

You all seemed to enjoy this interaction, but the next morning at breakfast Allie told you that you were not to play with the servant's children again and they were told not to come onto the house lawn. Privately you kids protested to me. Why couldn't Allison and his brother and sister play with you? I told you that most white people in South Africa thought it was better if black and white people were kept separate.

I found living in a society of entrenched inequality unsettling. Allie kept keys to lock the pantry to prevent theft by the cook, Bahati, who lived in a room next to the laundry behind the garage. Her daughter lived too far away to visit more than every few months.

I enjoyed the luxury of not having to cook or clean the kitchen or our bedroom, but I never got used to the presence of someone like a shadow in the background ready to respond to any request.

Although whites were a minority of the population, they formed the government which ruled with an iron grip, incarcerating dissenters like Nelson Mandela. It was like a miracle that after he was released from prison, he became the first black president when the African National Congress formed government after a series of negotiations in the early 1990s.

You, Jamie and Megan loved sitting in the back of Rex's buckie, what we call a ute, and calling out the few Zulu words of greeting that Garth had taught you.

'Sawubona,' you all called, waving at the children along the roadside. Then you added, 'Unjaniwena?' much to the delight of the children, who probably didn't often have white children interacting with them, especially in their local language. 'Sawubona,' they called back, waving. Rex didn't comment, but I wondered what he thought. His face was serious but neither approving nor disapproving.

We visited Garth's old school, which was an hour and a half drive from the farm. There were acres of grounds and two-storeyed red brick buildings framing a quadrangle with a fountain in the middle and soft, green not-to-be-walked on grass. Leading off from the quad was the library with its statues of philosophers and writers and the panelled dining hall with its long wooden tables. The chapel where students attended daily services was prominent too.

We wandered around the immaculately tended green lawns dotted with massive English oaks. A sign near the outdoor swimming pool read DO NOT THROW ACORNS INTO THE POOL.

'What was it like at this school?' you asked your dad.

'Tough,' he said. 'The senior boys beat us if we didn't do what they asked.'
'What sort of things?'
'Clean their shoes, iron their shirts and other stuff.'
'How often did you see Allie and Rex?'
'Three times a year during school holidays.'

Next we drove two days to Johannesburg to stay with Garth's school friend Malcolm and his family. Just before lunch you children followed the others to go and wash your hands. I walked past the bathroom. A young servant girl was standing beside the basin and you children were all lined up behind it. 'What are you doing?' I asked you.

'We're waiting for Abilla to wash our hands.'
'You can wash your own hands.'
'Here, the servant washes our hands,' you said.

Over the next few days, other old friends of Garth's invited us out. There were morning teas, lunches, dinners and drinks. Socialising was fun but relentless. 'Who do you get to cook?' the women would ask. 'Who does your laundry? Who cleans the house? Who looks after the children when you go to tennis?'

'I do,' I would say, and they would always be astonished.

Then the friends would compare the shortcomings of their servants. This topic was inexhaustible to them. I enjoyed their lively company and listened with interest to them discussing a different way of life to mine. I wonder if you chatted to Malcolm's children about things you did in Australia?

* * *

Malcolm's mother, who was also Allie's best friend, visited one day. She was sitting in the garden and held out a decorated open tin to Megan.

'Would you like a sweetie?' she asked, smiling. Did Megan smile in return and eagerly accept this kind offer? If she hadn't been asked to be friendly and polite to many strangers every day I'm sure that is what she would have done.

Now she stuck out her tongue in June's face. I looked on horrified as June laughed and said, 'What a pretty tongue.'

When I told Allie, she groaned that she wished it hadn't been June that Megan was so rude to.

George, the same man whose private game reserve your dad had stayed at as a boy, was an old army friend of Rex's. He kindly offered us his beach house at Plettenberg Bay. Your dad was thrilled at the thought of showing us this beautiful part of the South African coastline.

The house was grander than we anticipated, with a view over the ocean to the horizon and direct access to the beach, only a minute's walk away. George had explained that a maid would come each day to make the beds and cook and clean. Maisie arrived soon after we did.

'If you agree,' she said, 'I would prefer to cook a hot dinner in the middle of the day. Could you get your own light meal in the evening?'

'Of course, that would be fine,' Garth and I said.

'And would you be kind enough to drive me home when I finish for the day?' It was a shock to see where Maisie lived in a shantytown of narrow dirt roads and makeshift tin shacks. I wondered if there was running water or sewerage.

Each day Garth would surf further and further out at the "whites-only" section of the beach. The area was legendary for sharks. We took to sitting on the shore watching out for him anxiously, especially when he disappeared behind a big wave.

At night we would all walk down to the beach after dark where fireflies lit up the bushes like a fairyland. One night, further down through the scrubby foreshore, we heard voices and saw dark figures sitting around a fire on the sand. Your dad explained that they were most likely homeless coloureds who had set up camp there. I was a bit fearful but your dad was unconcerned, assuring me that they were harmless. Your dad seemed to me very brave in his familiar surroundings.

Do you remember us—but not your dad—being scared on a trip to

Lotheni Nature Reserve in the Drakensberg Mountains? We were all standing on the rocky ledge at a waterfall watching the water cascade thunderously over the edge. A troop of baboons were frolicking around near us on the ridge. Suddenly a young baboon jumped up on Jamie from behind and knocked him to the ground. Then it grabbed his cap and ran off. Jamie clutched his head.

'Give that back,' thundered Garth, who ran after it. 'Get in the car,' he yelled back to us, 'and wind up the windows, quick, or they'll jump in.'

Robbie, remember how terrified we all were as we scrambled into the car as fast as we could and wound up the windows? We watched scared as the young baboon reared up menacingly, flashing its long sharp teeth, but Garth, undeterred, snatched at Jamie's cap, tearing it out of the baboon's hands. Then the other baboons gathered around the younger one as if ready to retaliate. We were so glad when your dad got back in behind the steering wheel. Then in a final act of defiance, a big male jumped up onto the bonnet just as we drove off, pressing his bottom, huge and red, against the windscreen. Garth swerved violently and it fell off.

At Lotheni we were shown to our house some distance away from the campgrounds. Remember our surprise when a young black man with a pile of frizzy hair appeared at the door? I must have looked puzzled.

'I'm Victor to look after you,' he said.

'What do you do?' I asked.

'I'll chop wood and light the fire. I'll cook your dinner and breakfast tomorrow…'

We were grateful for the fire but I had planned to serve us all baked beans on toast so I said he could go home. Victor looked surprised and pleased.

The next morning he returned, clearly excited with white glitter all over the top of his hair. Megan begged to touch it. Obligingly he leant down for her. He couldn't say it in English but when he pointed outside we saw that it was snowing. This was the first time you children had seen snow and you all rushed out in your pyjamas.

'We're building a snowman,' you called out excitedly, plunging your fingers into the icy ground. I wish we hadn't stopped you by calling you inside to get dressed, suggesting you build it after breakfast.

'That's how you get chilblains,' your dad said, and I remembered how he'd told us stories of being forced to run barefoot around the school oval on frosty mornings.

That morning at Lotheni, the snow melted fast and after breakfast, there was too little left to make a snowman.

* * *

Garth had twice phoned the construction company back in Australia to extend his time off work so that our trip lasted not just five weeks but over two months. Driving back to Allie and Rex's place on our second last day in South Africa, do you remember how you pointed to a woman sitting in some grass on the side of the road? An African woman in a colourful dress was seated comfortably on the ground, weaving a hat.

'What's that lady doing? Can we have a look?' you asked.

We stopped to admire the woman's skill in twisting the coloured straws around the shapes she wanted, and we bought one of her large baskets and a hat, cone-shaped like so many Africans wear.

The next day we said goodbye to Allie at the farm and then Rex drove us to the station at Pietermaritzburg where we caught the overnight train to Johannesburg. You children were all so excited. Do you remember? Our cabin was spotlessly clean with two double bunks and a cot big enough for Megan. We all snuggled down under the crisp sheets and thick blankets, rocked asleep by the train's motion.

All too soon the overhead speaker was announcing that Johannesburg was the next stop. We grabbed our luggage and tumbled off the train. Garth and Jamie were immediately lost from sight in the crowd. I struggled to keep you and Megan close to me amongst the throng of tall blacks, pressing in all around us.

I stopped a large woman wrapped in a blanket and asked her for directions. In English, she explained that we were in the Johannesburg station for blacks. The station for whites was the next one, but she said we could walk there and pointed the way.

The black commuters were quiet and solemn, all heading off to work at six o'clock in the morning. The butchers' shops were open, doing a brisk trade. Large cuts of meat were hanging in the windows. There was also a shop open selling blankets. I held Megan's hand tight. You had your arms wrapped around our large basket full of souvenirs, trying to keep up.

We all finally got to the station for whites, where we should have alighted, only to find it eerily deserted. There was no-one around but us. The shops here had elaborate window displays of luxury items, perfumes, jewellery and designer clothes. I wondered what time they opened. Outside, the early morning air was fresh. Garth hailed a taxi to the airport.

28

Brisbane Then Eimeo

In Brisbane, your dad endured working in the main office by tendering for jobs anywhere else in Queensland.

'As soon as we win one, we'll move,' he said.

It took two years, during which Grandma came down on the bus from Bill's farm several times to stay during winter, leaving Grandpa at the farm.

For one term you walked by yourself to Kenmore Public School which was around the corner from our house. You didn't talk about being in the classroom or lessons or the teacher. You never brought home any school books. You only talked about the fun games at lunchtime and the names of friends you played with.

Jamie refused to return to kindergarten after only attending for three days.

Your dad and I made an offer to buy the Kenmore house we rented and did the conveyancing on the purchase ourselves. He did the paperwork and I trundled off to the Titles Office to check the title several times and to the bank to take out a loan.

It was a brick house on a slab, had three bedrooms and a huge poinciana on the front lawn, with very little garden. A wide easement along the back was a playground for you kids. It was comfortable for us and an excellent house to rent out when we left.

Towards the end of 1980, your dad came home with the news that the tender for the construction of a sugar-receiving terminal in Mackay had been successful. I told Grandma that we were heading north again. We would be living more than two thousand kilometres away from Melbourne. 'At least it's not as far as Townsville,' she said.

Garth asked Ken, an engineering colleague, to scout around for accommodation for us preferably near the ocean. Ken drove us to Eimeo, a tiny township twenty minutes drive north of Mackay.

'Sorry, mate,' he said, 'but this was the only rental house on the books anywhere near the sea. Rental properties are as rare as hen's teeth around Mackay, especially on the coast.'

We all got out of the car and stood staring at a small, shabby, white timber shack. Where was the area of secure lawn for you kids to play on? The clothesline? There was no garden at all and surely we were too many to be comfortable in a dwelling so small?

'What do you think?' Ken said, looking at me. 'It's furnished.'

'I'm dubious but I'll have a look inside and then decide,' I said.

Inside was even more basic than I'd imagined. We walked straight into an open-plan kitchen with a dining area and two couches in one corner. Off this area was a very small bedroom. Squeezed into it was a bunk and small bed for you children and off this a toilet and shower. At the top of a narrow, circular metal staircase was a larger room with a balcony which could be the master bedroom.

Out the front door was a narrow dirt track with the grandiose name, Sunset Boulevarde. This house was number four. Across the road a patch of green grass led to a strip of golden sand which curved around a wide bay bordering a glittering aqua sea. Further out, across the water, were several islands.

After a glance through the door, you raced across the grass and sand to the water, followed by Jamie and Megan. 'Are we going to live here?' you asked running back, clearly excited.

'We might just make it work,' I said to Ken.

'We'd better take it then,' said Garth.

'Until something better comes up,' I added.

After we moved in, my initial concern about having no yard was dismissed within minutes when you went out onto the beach with Jamie and Megan. At first, I could always see you on the sand but as it all became familiar and you, at seven years old, took to looking after the younger ones so responsibly, you would venture further along the beach to the rocky headland in search of shells.

Stories of swimmers suffering searing pain, and even death, from the stings of large box jellyfish, initially filled us with fear so before going into the water, we completely covered up. This was the only time, in or out of the water, in our years of living on Sunset Bay, that you ever wore so much clothing. We would all get dressed in long-sleeved shirts, long pants and socks whenever we went swimming until, after some weeks, we turned into blasé locals and swam in the clear, cool water just wearing our togs. The local fishermen reassured us that they knew when the jellies were around and that, if they ever spotted them, they would give us a warning. We only had to be cautious between certain summer months and even then, they said, the appearance of the jellies depended on the tides.

How deliciously refreshing the water felt on hot skin. It was clear right to the sandy bottom, but still it was difficult to spot a jellyfish's long, thin, venom-laced tentacles.

Your dad took Sundays off work, and we enjoyed being together as a family. All five of us could sit on the bench seats in our canoe without being squashed. Garth and I would sit at either end with you children in the middle and dip the oars deep and slow into the water. The boat would slink silently up the Eimeo Creek through the mangroves at the end of our beach.

We would stop and sit quietly watching large greenish-brown crabs scuttle across the mud or be surprised by small mud-coloured crabs that were camouflaged until they moved. The grey mud had a distinctively pungent smell. Snails crawled along slowly over it too. Occasionally silent unseen birds would take flight through the branches above and startle us. One time, a lizard high up in a tree trunk just above our heads dropped into the water, shattering the silence with an explosive boom. It never occurred to us that this was a perfect breeding ground for crocodiles.

The five of us would often wade across the creek channel to Bucasia at low tide and walk along the curved flat beach. This was the same beach we had enjoyed on weekends from the dust bowl of Dysart. We would again marvel when thousands of soldier crabs suddenly appeared and marched across the wet sand, then if disturbed, just as suddenly corkscrew down into holes, leaving behind neat piles of tiny muddy balls.

But it was only you who spotted the unusual shells. There would be cone shells in hues of red and brown, which, if they still contained live sea creatures, had to be handled with care because they were venomous. Some shells were two centimetres long, some were twenty. There were glossy cowries with white or brown spots, sand dollars, flat and round just like thin white coins with a star pattern on top, and spiral orangey-pink conch shells with flared lips. Your favourites were left by the sea urchins—large, round purple or green shells covered in white dots that looked as if they had been glued on.

One day your dad arrived home unusually early and ran into the house.

'A cyclone is heading our way,' he yelled excitedly, straining to be heard against the already strong buffeting wind.

'What do we do?' I asked anxiously, having no idea what we were about to face.

'Shut all the windows and doors. Everything outside must be brought inside.'

You caught your dad's excitement and rushed out to lug in furniture, bikes, boxes, beach towels. We watched and listened to the wind getting stronger as it bent the trees and lashed at the waves. To your and your dad's disappointment and my relief, the cyclone dissipated offshore.

Sunset Bay was a magical beach at any time of day, but although the sparkling aqua sea was dimmer at dusk, the sunsets were spectacular, breathtaking, and we never tired of exclaiming over their beauty as the sky coloured in brilliant red and orange hues.

29

1 Sunset Boulevarde

A year after arriving at Eimeo we bought the house at 1 Sunset Boulevarde, two doors along the beach from our rental, but now no road separated our house from the seashore. It was on a three-quarter-acre block, three times the size, with a dam out the back belonging to the Beachcomber Motel next door.

As the new owners we were told that we must build a separate access as we could no longer use the motel's entrance.

'Keep going,' yelled Garth, as he waved me further back with one hand while holding the theodolite in the other. He stood on the dry bank, urging me to walk backwards, further and deeper into the dark, possibly snake-infested dam. Water lapped my knees as I peered into the dark surface for wriggling creatures.

'Let's change places, you hold the level, and I'll do the readings,' I said.

He explained how to make measurements on the theodolite, which he'd borrowed from work.

'Robbie would enjoy doing this,' I said.

You then read and wrote down the levels Garth needed to construct the new road. Do you remember doing that?

When the dam flooded after torrential tropical rain, fortunately not coinciding with a king tide, you took the canoe out and soon friends filled it up. You clung onto overhanging branches before jumping into the water yelling and singing. You had all had swimming lessons in Townsville but because Megan was only three, I asked you to watch her. You nodded, and I knew you would. Once I asked you if you ever saw snakes in the dam.

'Oh, yes, they just swim past,' you said.

During the first load of washing I did, I lifted the lid of the machine when it had filled with water and was startled to see the top covered in little black creatures.

'What are these?' I demanded showing them to you.

'Oh, they're just cane toad tadpoles from the dam. You said we could kill cane toads so we filled out pockets with them.'

I asked you, in future, to first empty your pockets into a bucket outside.

On this block all that separated the house from the sea was a patch of front lawn shaded by a eucalypt, a wodyetia palm, a Queensland umbrella tree and a silky oak, and then golden sand stretching out towards the ever-turquoise ocean. We owned the land up to the mean high-water mark, one of the very few properties with a title like this in the whole of Australia.

One night, I heard a gurgling, splashing sound and got up in the dark to investigate. To my astonishment, the sound was of waves lapping over our front doorstep. This was the king tide of North Queensland I'd been told about, a five-metre rise that in winter came at night.

The next morning, you and the others gleefully all jumped off the front step into knee-high water, delightedly kicking water at each other, while your dad and I watched. Then you stepped through the front door, soaked.

On other mornings, in other months, the high tide could be a hundred metres out and the sand seemed to go on forever until it joined up with the beach on the other side of the bay.

The house itself, though small, seemed spacious after the rental. Your dad installed an outside shower hoping to reduce the quantity of sand we all walked inside. We splurged on a big outdoor timber dining table and long matching stools with backrests and put them under the trees out on the grass.

We ate most of our meals outside from then on, sometimes surrounded by a ring of silent brown cane toads and watchful greenish frogs. The menu almost always included homemade bread, and tomatoes and cucumbers that were growing in the hydroponics planted by the previous owner. I replaced most of the tomato plants and grew carnations instead, selling them as single blooms outside the Eimeo pub on Valentine's Day after you'd helped me wire the stems because the flower heads were so heavy.

You were the first to warn us of the taipan that lived under the log we stepped over separating the grass from the sand. It was long, brown and shiny and slithered under the log fast, you said. Taipans are the second-most venomous snakes in the world and can be aggressive, so we looked carefully before putting a foot down from then on. The snake never troubled us again. More dangerous still were the stonefish you children spotted playing on the rocks near the sand. The deadliest of all fish, they would lie still, camouflaged amongst the rocks, their sharp spines loaded with venom. We discussed how you had to keep looking where you walked, especially as none of you wore shoes on the beach.

After roaming the neighbourhood for the first time you and the others came home with stains down your shirts and faces, and yellow fibres in your teeth. I asked what you'd been eating.

'Just mangoes,' you said. 'They're all over the ground along Mango Avenue.'

And the day you returned with red around your mouths I asked again.

'We found a wild tomato bush.'

Remember how on most afternoons I'd asked you all to have a rest and read a book, but you would sneak out of your bedroom with Jamie and Megan in tow? Your room had an external door and Bouchie, who was your age and lived further along the beach, would have been calling out to you. He couldn't understand why you had to be home for lunch at a particular time on Sundays.

'I just make a jam sammich for meself when I get home,' he used to say. 'Why don't you?'

There was a little park next to the mangroves where the blossom from the tea trees gave a pungent, sickening smell that made me retch. It didn't bother you or your little gang who often played under the poinciana tree, hidden by its drooping branches.

One afternoon, I could smell cigarette smoke on you. You told me that Bouchie had stolen a packet of his dad's cigarettes and shared them with you all on the beach under the poinciana.

'Not Megan too?' I asked.

'I smoked too,' said my three-year-old proudly.

You said it made you feel sick, and the experience put you off smoking for good.

Another day you came rushing home yelling, 'There's a shark on the beach.' You raced down the sand with me following. Sure enough a sand shark had washed up. We checked to make sure it was dead.

Every day you roamed the beach, especially around the rocky headlands and around to the next beach. One day you and Bouchie and Jamie staggered home lugging heavy staghorns.

'Where did you find them?' I was horrified, wondering if they had been stolen.

'We found them on trees near the mangroves behind the next beach and thought you'd like them,' you said.

'Thank you, but don't get any more. They belong on the native trees,' I said.

We tied the booty to our trees near the sand.

Recently, Jamie told me about the yellow and black sea snake you had found trapped in a shallow pool when the tide was going out on Eimeo Beach. With a stick, you and he and Bouchie had flicked it onto the sand then tried to get it into a long-necked, brown beer bottle you had found nearby. I've read that sea snakes are venomous but they only bite if they are provoked!

During our second year at Sunset Bay, you and Jamie attended the Eimeo Public School. You walked around the dam and up our new road to meet Bouchie at the bus stop on Mango Avenue wearing shorts, a T-shirt and hat.

Some days Jamie wore shoes, but you never did. Your feet ran over the roughest, sharpest surfaces and on the bare, dusty ground at school playing rugby league—or was it soccer?

If it had rained, you'd float sticks down the gutters. You never mentioned what you did in the classroom, or bring any books home, but you delighted in lunchtime games.

One day, you came home and told me that you liked Bouchie's mum. I found myself saying, 'But Robbie, she's only a barmaid at the pub.'

You looked at me hard then and said, 'I don't think you're very nice, Mum,' and walked out the door, leaving me feeling ashamed.

I have often thought about how you as an eight-year-old pulled me up for my judgment of Leanne, and how much what you thought mattered to me. You said this before she caught you and Bouchie and Jamie at Mango Avenue, lying down on the double lines playing chicken, jumping off the road at the last minute when a car approached. Leanne gave you all a roasting.

The game she didn't see and that I heard about later was you jumping on the school bus's back bumper while it turned around and jumping off before it sped up.

When you lost your bus pass, remember how you cut a cigarette packet to the same size and copied Jamie's with ink and coloured pencils to appear the same, at least enough to pass a glancing look from the driver?

One Easter holiday we spent at Newry, an island in the Whitsundays north of Cape Hillsborough. A rough dirt track led us to the jetty where we were attacked savagely by sandflies. A group of people, as well as us, waited there for the launch to take us to Newry. We were unimpressed when a small dingy chugged up.

The driver, tanned and lean, introduced himself as Ron and told us to hop in. I think we all wondered how many trips this was going to take. Ron yelled at us to hop in when we hesitated. Yes, all of you, he repeated loudly.

We squished up together and children sat on the adults' knees. Ron said to your dad, 'Give 'er a push mate.' Garth heaved to get the overladen dingy that was now wedged in the sand into the water, then jumped in.

Any apprehension about being overcrowded on a small vessel at sea was overcome by the sheer beauty and variety of the life under the crystal clear water as we slowly chugged along. We each excitedly pointed at schools of tiny orange fish or silver thin ones and others close under the surface.

Newry was the first coral cay we'd visited. You were the only one of us who could walk barefoot on the sharp crushed-coral beach, which was glaringly white in the sun.

Our cabin was basic, but meals were communal around a primitive barbecue. We ate potatoes, salad and red emperor caught that day while we listened to sea adventures by the yachtsmen who had sailed to Newry from Tonga and beyond. They spoke of their adventures sailing in storms or being becalmed. Their obvious love of the sea was intoxicating.

Then they exclaimed about the number of sharks they'd seen in the water at the Newry beach, so of course we were worried when your dad swam there the next morning, but he emerged unscathed and looked more refreshed than the rest of us. You wanted to go for a swim too, but I said no.

Our visit to Newry wasn't the luxury holiday I'd anticipated but a simple, relaxing one highlighted by our privileged glimpses of the sheer beauty of the pristine, vibrant Barrier Reef waters.

* * *

Sometimes on Friday evening we would drive to Garth's work for happy hour, then have dinner at Al Pappa's for your favourite, spag bol or pizzas. After leaving there one evening, Garth swerved to settle a pile of ledgers on the back shelf of the car and was pulled over by the police, who'd spotted this erratic driving. The breathalyser didn't work, so he was taken to the station with the rest of us following.

Remember how nervous we were at being kept waiting for so long? It wasn't like the fun Sue and I had in a Northern Ireland police station.

On many Sunday afternoons, we'd all stroll up the hill to the Eimeo pub. I still think it has the best-located beer garden in Australia with its one hundred and eighty degree view over the Pacific. From the beer garden, we could see Barrier Reef islands, some close and some just dots in the distance.

A band would play 1970s rock loudly and the crowd, mostly workers from the coal mines and the cane farms, would shout and swear even louder to be heard over it. You would crawl under the tables with Jamie and Megan and often find coins, and once you found a note. Your dad and I enjoyed the pub's casual atmosphere and it only took five minutes to walk there.

Garth worked long hours but occasionally he and I would sit on the beach enjoying the cool of the evening, drinking a beer and gazing at the sun setting behind the hills on the distant curve of the bay.

Now after two years the sugar receiving mill was complete and Garth looked forward to another type of project with different challenges in a new location. The only time you were ever sad at Eimeo and one of the few times you ever cried, Robbie, was when I told you that we were leaving.

'Do we have to go?' you had asked. 'Why do we have to leave?'

'Dad has a job in New South Wales,' I said. 'We need to move south.'

'Couldn't Dad go and we stay here?'

'No, we all have to go together. We will never sell the house,' I told you. 'We'll come back one day.'

I lent our beach furniture to friends who kindly agreed to look after it until we returned. It shouldn't be too long, a few years at the most, I told them. I asked you if you minded if we left your shell collection behind too, to minimise the stuff we needed to pack. You seemed too sad about the move to care. So it was left and I have never seen such a fine, unusual collection since.

Sadly, we never did return.

30

Scone in The Hunter Valley

After five years of acclimatising in North Queensland's tropical temperatures, an added shock after leaving Eimeo was having our teeth chattering uncontrollably when we stepped off the plane at Cessnock in the Hunter Valley. Do you remember how we could hardly speak for the cold that hit us?

We had a few days before our rental in Scone was ready so we went shopping in Tamworth for much-needed warmer clothing and, for the first time, school uniforms. I wonder if you remember your experience buying shoes? The shop assistant looked at your feet that had gone unshod for years.

'No,' he said, shaking his head doubtfully, 'I don't think we'll have anything wide enough.'

Your feet, resting on a firm cushion, were soon surrounded by boxes that appeared one after the other in quick succession. The assistant, a pleasant young man took the lid off each one, opened them patiently at first, revealing yet another pair of black leather school shoes with laces. I waited for him to tell you to stand up and walk around, to feel if they were comfortable, but it never got to that. No matter how hard he tried, he couldn't squeeze one shoe on. Finally, exasperated, he brought out one last box and throwing it down, said, 'Try them on yourself.' He walked stiffly away.

Scone Primary accepted soft black sneakers and the pair in that last box fitted. Jamie and Megan's feet managed to fit into the widest black leather school shoes. We bought jumpers and parkas which you each wore out of the shop. We bought pyjamas and dressing gowns too. Finally, you all stopped shivering. Your dad and I got out the woollen jumpers and socks that we had kept in storage for years.

Garth would be managing a big construction site forty-five minutes' drive away. He was excited about the prospect of this new project. Not only was the design and structure of cooling towers new to him, so were the work team and the environment.

Mac Abbott, our cheerful, gentlemanly landlord met us on arrival at 95 Waverley Street.

'I've moved into the cottage across the road. It's a much better size for one person,' he said. 'This bigger house needs a family to fill it up.'

If we could have shifted this Scone house to our block at Eimeo, we would have had the perfect house in an idyllic location. Mac's home was charming. Built in 1910, it was a rambling country house with wings added, each of which had a bathroom and an area for reading or watching television. High ceilings throughout made it seem even more spacious but, we discovered, difficult to heat in winter.

The large chandelier over the dining room table sparkled brightly after Grandpa washed it during a visit, following Grandma's instructions. The house had three fireplaces, each of them decorated with hand painted tiles, and an antique four-poster bed Mac left behind, where visitors slept.

For the first time you children could each have your own room but you chose to stay together. There was a brief time when you moved to a separate bedroom, but you only lasted a week before moving back to the large room at the front of the house that you shared with Jamie and Megan. Then Jamie tried sleeping alone in an enclosed verandah space but he, too, soon moved back.

The bedroom you three shared had an open fireplace, which you all had strict instructions never to light.

You slept in a single bed. Jamie chose the top bunk, from which he frequently fell out with a loud bang, on one occasion frightening burglars who had got into the kitchen.

The stained-glass front door opened onto a hallway, which was easily wide enough for the piano. You enjoyed playing the piano after Anne, the music teacher who lived next door, came in to give you your first lessons. She remarked on how quickly you learnt music and asked if you were good at maths.

Garth and I loved our grand bedroom in this house. It was furnished with huge old timber wardrobes leaving plenty of room for our king-size bed. A modern ensuite had been added and also a closed-in garden room where we could sit in peaceful privacy.

At the back fence was a huge mulberry tree hanging over a large old shed and workshop. Next to it was a plot for a vegetable garden, and an enclosure for Khaki Campbell ducks, which we began breeding after a friend gave us some eggs and Mac lent us a broody hen to sit on them.

There was a grassed area big enough for the cricket and footy and mud wrestling you boys both loved and shared with friends at your combined birthday parties.

'What food would you like for your party?' I asked you each year.

You always answered, 'Spag bol and chocolate bavarian please mum.'

Jamie was happy with your choice, but had his own birthday cake.

Grandma and Grandpa bought you and Jamie Kuwahara BMX bikes, just like the ones that magically take flight in the chase scene in the movie *E.T.* On the quiet, wide streets of Scone, your bikes gave you the same sort of freedom that a car gives an adult. The next year, for Megan's fifth birthday they gave her a blue Malvern Star bike with a white wicker basket featuring fluoro flowers on the front.

How delighted you kids were with these bikes. You could ride to school by yourselves, and visit mates. On some weekends, we all rode to a friend's farm ten kilometres out and played tennis there.

One day, remember how you three came in each carrying a tiny puppy?

A black and white border collie bitch had jumped off the back of a truck going through town just before giving birth to a litter of five under the house next door. My kind neighbour was feeding them Weet-Bix and warm milk, but didn't want to own any of them.

'Please can we keep one?' you pleaded.

'Look at this one, Mum, it's so little,' Jamie said.

'And this fluffy one,' said Megan.

'I love dogs but every year or so we spend several weeks in a motel between your dad's jobs,' I said. 'We couldn't manage those moves with a dog.'

Undeterred, every afternoon you three children would carry in a different pup. Finally, I said, 'If we had a dog it must be small, have short hair and it must stay outdoors.'

From then, you only brought in the smallest two, one of which had short hair. It waddled on its little stumpy legs into the formal living room and piddled on the carpet. Inexplicably, my resistance melted and we then had a puppy that you named Buster. He was the colour of a dingo, his eyes were a soft brown and he learnt commands quickly. He slept on the back verandah wearing one of Jamie's sleeveless woollen jumpers on cold nights. He became my responsibility to train and occasionally incur the anger of the council ranger, because I never had him on a lead. Your dad also had enjoyed having a pet dog as a child, so he liked having Buster too.

* * *

As you know, as often as possible your dad would suggest a weekend at the coast. He'd pack the trailer with mattresses and tents and we'd head off over the Barrington Tops to Seal Rocks.

In summer, we'd hop from foot to foot, the sand burning the soles of our feet while we set up the camp site. We'd race down and plunge into the surf for instant relief. Buster barked madly as he chased seagulls along the firm sand. Your dad would encourage you three children out further into the water to body surf the waves with him back to shore. You, Jamie and Megan all developed a love of the ocean and later all took to board surfing.

In the late afternoon, we'd take chips, soft drinks and beer to sit on the sand and watch the sun set before making a campfire to cook our chops and heat up vegetarian sausages from a tin.

Other times, over a long weekend, we'd stay at a house near Soldiers Point which was owned by Mac's daughter. We spent hours staring into the colourful rock pools at low tide, poking our fingers into the anemones which curled around them.

My favourite weekend place was the Barrington Guesthouse in Barrington Tops, where we'd find tawny frogmouths. Do you remember how they perched on a shelf in the barn looking more like wood carvings than birds? We'd walk through the forests and maybe take a dip in the river, where the water was always so cold.

If your dad worked on Saturday, we'd have a picnic along the Hunter River on Sunday. I loved the family being together like this but maybe you would have preferred riding your bike with friends?. Garth and I would read while you would all throw rocks into the water for Buster to bring back, which is how he wore his teeth down to stumps, or you'd make dams or float down the river in tyre tubes.

One Sunday morning, your dad said excitedly, 'The Hunter's in flood. Let's take the canoe out.' We couldn't find the paddles and realised that we had probably left them at Eimeo.

'Okay, I'll use our shovels instead,' he said.

We parked on the riverbank and looked down at the raging water as it carried along sticks, boxes and even a tree trunk.

'You won't put the canoe in that,' I said, but Garth couldn't hear me over the roar of the river. He was already out of the car heaving the heavy canoe off the car roof rack.

'Come on, bring the shovels,' he shouted to you and Jamie.

He headed down the bank and told you and Jamie to hop in. You both sat watching the water rush downstream, taking along everything in its path at the same furious pace. Just as your dad was pushing out, you and Jamie both said you didn't want to go. Cranky, Garth pushed a shovel into the side of the bank, trying to steady the boat enough for you to get out. You both somehow managed to scramble out just before your dad accidentally dropped the shovel into the water. The canoe, still carrying Garth in it, hurtled on.

In a moment, he was gone. Where would he and the canoe be when we saw him again? I bundled you all back into the car and we drove as far as we could towards the bridge, hoping that's where he might be able to stop. Your dad survived, the canoe stayed intact, and he berated you and Jamie for chickening out.

Do you remember that before Megan started school she accompanied me to the Scone Red Cross cattle and horse yards canteen, where I volunteered once or twice a month?

'What do you do there?' you had asked, the first time we went.

'Farmers come to sell or buy sheep or cattle, sometimes horses,' I replied. 'After they unload their animals and before the auction begins they come in for a cup of tea. I boil water in a large urn and make sandwiches. There's a choice of plain silverside, silverside with pickles, silverside with tomato sauce or silverside with salad. No-one ever asks for anything else. I heat up pies in the oven. After the sales, they come in again before loading their stock and heading home.'

'Did you bring any leftover pies home today?' you would ask, hopefully, each time I served there.

* * *

After Megan started school, I was free, for the first time in nine years, to work. Do you remember when I announced to the family that I had enrolled in a Postgraduate Diploma in Financial Management at the University of New England? Your dad brought you all up to Armidale during one of my compulsory residencies.

After graduating with that diploma and taking on extra subjects to qualify potentially as a chartered accountant, I drove an hour to Singleton and worked in an accountant's office three days a week. Remember how the Nissan Pulsar got pitted from coal flying out from the trucks on the road?

On the other two days, I taught numeracy and literacy skills at Scone TAFE, and English to the Japanese wives of the computer experts working at the Bayswater Power Station. I enjoyed this stimulation.

By the time we moved to Scone, you, at the age of eight, had mastered basic sums and geometry, spelling, and writing stories and drawing. The biggest immediate challenge you had when you started at Scone Primary part way through Year 4 was not about the content but the process.

Do you remember how in your first week, you came home and told me that the class was asked to write a story but the bell went before you'd finished? At the sound, the other kids all downed pens and stood to leave. You didn't know what to do. Should you finish your story, which was what you had always done at home, or stop with it unfinished and go out to play with the others? It was a genuine dilemma for you. I said you had better go out with the others and finish your story at home.

In your Year 6, an Australia-wide test was administered across schools to determine students' proficiency in particular skills. Your teacher excitedly told me that you scored in the top one to two per cent in every skill. He had never had a student score so highly. In a Hunter Valley writing competition you were selected to participate in a writers camp and came home a week later with a book of poems you'd written. You won the school maths prize.

Garth expected his next job to be in Brisbane. You would be starting high school.

There were long waiting lists for admittance to private schools and old boys were given preference. I travelled up in a bus and presented your report full of A-pluses to the headmaster at Brisbane's Church of England Grammar School and because he was so impressed with your report, not only did he accept you, he accepted Jamie too.

Two months later, Garth came home and announced that we were not going to Brisbane after all. We were moving to Sydney instead. We just weren't sure when.

You sat an exam in the hope of winning a scholarship because none of the top private Sydney schools would accept such a late enrolment without one. You won a full scholarship to the Scots College and were offered a place at the selective Sydney Grammar School but we chose Knox Grammar, without a scholarship. You were offered a place at Knox because you'd topped its English scholarship exam. It was an impressive school that felt more familiar because we passed it on our drives from Scone to inner Sydney and we knew a boarder who seemed happy there.

On the first day Dr Paterson, the headmaster, explained that the new boarding house for Year 7 hadn't been completed in time, so you'd be accommodated temporarily in the old assembly hall. I left seeing your pale face looking around as you calmly took it all in, the bed you'd been allocated, the desk, the chest of drawers for your clothes and books, the boys who knew each other all chatting excitedly in groups and the few others like you sitting alone, quiet. The scene looked like a wartime hospital without nurses. I wondered how I'd manage not being able to contact you for six weeks—a school rule.

I gave Grandma and Grandpa regular updates on your school experience. Grandma had been a boarder when she studied for Year 12, then went to the Teachers' College. Your uncle Bill had been a boarder at an agricultural college at fifteen. Your dad had been your age when he started boarding, but Sue, your godmother, was only seven when she was sent away to school. They had all survived and I knew you would make the most of this new experience. In the past you had always settled quickly into new environments.

Just before the six weeks were up, Matron rang to tell me you were in the school hospital and had been since yesterday. I listened as she said it was nothing to worry about, you were not sick, just tired, and after sleeping for two days and nights, you were fine. I asked you about it.

'Did you put your pyjamas on?' I asked.

'No, Matron said to hop into bed as you are,' you said.

'You took your blazer and shoes off?'

'No, Matron said hop in as you are, so I did.'

I pictured you sleeping in full school uniform, including blazer and shoes, for two full days.

'What did you do in the evenings?' I asked.

'I went back to the boarding house and slept all night, on both nights.'

The next time I heard from Matron, two months later, you were back in the hospital with measles. This time you wore pyjamas.

We were all excited when you came home during the holidays, bringing all the latest schoolboy expressions and swear words which rapidly spread around Scone Primary. Jamie and Megan devoured your stories about boarding school life, the teachers and the other boarders. You rattled off the names of all the stations between Wahroonga and Central after taking one return train trip on your first "Saturday leave".

I asked about school subjects. In English, the teacher had asked each boy to write about himself and said she was delighted that you had so much to say. I was intrigued because you never usually talked about yourself.

You continued piano lessons with an elderly lady, at her house in Wahroonga. Many months later you were startled to realise that she was totally blind and described in detail how she moved around without stumbling. I proudly listened to you perform when I attended a recital by her pupils, in her living room. Knox allocated a music room for your twice-weekly practice. You also studied music as a subject and your dad helped you with an assignment to make an instrument from wood.

You loved playing soccer and the camaraderie of the boys, all your age, at the boarding house.

During your second year as a boarder, your dad was offered the major role of project manager for the construction of a huge building in the city. For several months at the start, he was away in Sydney most weeks while I stayed in Scone with Jamie and Megan.

We had enjoyed settling into Scone over five years, the longest stint we'd ever had anywhere. We'd had time to settle into the community and feel a part of it. School, work and family Sundays had become routine. But now Garth became increasingly distant and distracted. He no longer visited you at school even though he drove right past. I even wondered if it would be better for us all to stay in Scone, where we had made firm friends and you were happy as a boarder.

'Garth, do you really want us to move to Sydney?' I asked him.

'Yes,' he said.

'Are you sure?'

'Yes, definitely,' he said.

I dreaded the prospect of living in a big city again, a city I didn't know and where I knew not a single person. The only light in my reluctance was you being close enough to see often.

I relied once more on Grandma and Grandpa's help in our biggest move yet. We had accumulated more stuff in this huge house, and we had a dog.

Over the next few weeks, we packed up Mac Abbott's house and relocated to a motel in Wahroonga, where we would stay for the first three weeks.

31

Unravelling in Sydney

It was May 1986 when Garth and I had bought the large, ramshackle, two-storey house with a big garden, only five minutes' drive away from the school. I was excited that you'd be living at home again and thought you would be too. But you told me gently that you enjoyed the boarding house and could you stay there as long as possible, please?

Later that year you only casually mentioned, as an aside, that you would be getting two academic prizes at speech night, to be held at the Opera House. Proud and excited, I phoned Garth at work and suggested that I book a table at a restaurant in the city for a celebratory meal beforehand.

'I can't leave work,' he said.

'But the speech night isn't for two weeks and it doesn't start until eight o'clock. You don't have to work until then, do you?'

'Yes I do, there's a lot on.'

After three phone calls during the day of Speech Night urging him to attend he reluctantly agreed to come. So, I boarded the train with his suit over my arm and his shoes in a bag. It was important to me that your dad and I were both there to celebrate your success. I couldn't wait to see you walk across that iconic stage.

Your dad's behaviour had changed since he had started working on the city construction project. He was exhausted from the pressure of the stressful job and working long hours. He had become distant and angered easily. At home we all started to walk on eggshells when he was around. He denied it when I asked if he was having an affair.

That was when I started crying a lot, Robbie, but not in front of him or you children. I often found myself weeping behind the steering wheel when I was driving alone.

Each day at the accounting firm, I interviewed clients in my office and sorted out issues for their businesses and tax returns. One day, John, my boss, was standing in my office doorway and asked me a question. I wouldn't look up from my desk to answer, because I didn't want him to see my eyes full of tears. It was better to be impolite than to try to explain why I was crying.

I needed help, so I went to see a GP. The doctor was kind and compassionate and said he could give me a referral to a specialist. Before he specified what specialist I thanked him, but said I thought that would be hopeless, and feeling helpless, I left the surgery still crying. I wondered if anyone could help me.

Early the next morning, my kind, friendly Texan next-door neighbour, Kay, and I were walking our dogs at the local park together when I burst into tears. I explained to her that I couldn't stop crying. Kay told me that she knew someone who could help me—a Christian Science practitioner. I had no idea what that was and no desire to turn to religion.

For the past thirty years, I had not gone to church. Nevertheless, when Kay made an appointment for me to meet Beverley at her Dee Why office, I felt it would be ungracious not to go. And I was desperate.

With some scepticism as to how this stranger could help me, I sobbed my way through the hour-long consultation but I was quiet by the time I left.

Beverley didn't say much, but she assured me that God loved me, adding that another name for God is Love. I wondered how God knew about my sadness, and how Beverley knew that God knew, but on the way home, I felt a surge of warmth and safety, and I have hardly cried since.

Beverley's guidance from that moment on helped me function as a mother of you, Jamie and Megan, as an accountant, and as a supportive wife to a husband who was behaving so uncharacteristically. She said there was good around me. I found that the more I looked for good, the more I experienced it. The more gratitude I expressed, the happier I felt, and my mind felt clearer to make decisions. I embraced a God who loved me unconditionally. Also, I was not answerable to anything or anyone, but my conscience. Disciplining my thinking proved invaluable. I tried to keep my thoughts in the present, not the past or future. I was experiencing positive outcomes, so I searched through my bookshelves and found the King James Bible my grandmother had given me when I was a young child. I studied it for comfort, wisdom and strength. I wanted to help your dad too, but for the few hours he was at home, he needed to sleep.

In what turned out to be your dad's and my last outing together, a wonderful encounter happened. Garth's work's Christmas party that year was held at Mt Victoria in the Blue Mountains. The next morning we went for a short bush walk and met two backpackers admiring the view. Tall, blonde, blue-eyed Svend and short, dark-haired, funny Hans, both from Denmark enjoyed chatting with us. They needed somewhere to stay in Sydney and I offered them our spare room at Wahroonga. They provided some welcome lightheartedness. They ate dinner with us through nights when your dad was often absent. They stayed with us for six weeks and worked as carpenters on a local building site. They were friendly, kind and wonderful with you children. You, especially loved playing basketball with them and slam dunking in the hoop on the tree out the front. Along with Jamie and Megan you would laugh as they kidded around, enjoying your company as they practised speaking English. For me, their cheerful presence was like a ray of sunshine.

On the Saturday morning after Svend and Hans had left Garth came into the laundry and said to me, 'I want us to go for a walk down to the park.'

'What, now?' I asked.

I pressed the start button on the machine for the second load of washing.

'Yes, now, I want to talk to you,' he said.

I was disturbed at the coldness in his voice. What couldn't he say in the kitchen? Why a walk to the park to say it? It must be serious. Is he extremely ill? It couldn't be an affair because he had denied that suggestion.

We were both quiet and tense on the short walk along Cliff Avenue.

At the oval, I was acutely aware of the vibrant red bottlebrushes flowering along the boundary fence, the loud buzzing of the bees alighting on them and the smell of the wattle. When Garth came out with the words that he was leaving us to go to live with his secretary, I found myself bodiless, floating, looking down at a scene of two people walking around the park, having a conversation. I knew it was Garth and me, but I felt separate, not involved. I could not be affected because, thank goodness, I was up above them. Whatever was going on down there had nothing to do with me. I heard the person who looked like me whisper, 'When?' and Garth replied next Saturday, unless I wanted him gone earlier.

Want him gone earlier? Of course, I didn't want him gone earlier. Was a week long enough for him to realise this had to be a mistake? I felt a surge of anger. However unsatisfactory our marriage had been at times, I thought we had always been friends.

Silent on the walk home, I was aware of my feet hitting the bitumen, heavily grounded, down to earth, no longer a mere observer. My head was exploding with shock. Questions pounded through my mind that needed answering urgently. Our relationship was intricate. Where to start? We had to tell you, Jamie and Megan, but how could we break it to you all gently, to lessen the potential impact? None of you should have your lives disrupted like this.

I was disbelieving. Everything Garth and I currently shared soared up in the air in an instant. Any order I had in my life had been flung into pieces somewhere out there in space. Would I recognise the crucial parts to catch and which ones to let drop? I had to protect you kids—that was my primary role.

Remember how you, Jamie and Megan followed us into the lounge room. Our expressions showed that this was serious as you all sat solemnly side-by-side on the couch, staring at us apprehensively.

'I'm moving out, to live somewhere else for a while,' your dad said.

Megan began to cry while Jamie held back tears. Your face, Rob, remained impassive.

'I'll still see you,' he said. It did not sound reassuring.

'Where are you moving to?' you asked, matter-of-factly.

'The other side of Sydney, an hour's drive away.'

The next week work colleagues of Garth's phoned me, disbelieving. Some expressed sadness and alarm that he was behaving in a way that seemed so out of character.

For me anger was followed by disbelief. His behaviour made no sense. So many years later I still find his actions then, bewildering.

You seemed to instinctively and immediately understand my deep grief at your dad's sudden departure. How grateful I was to have your quiet, gentle, mature, supportive presence.

Garth had said that he'd take away the rest of his clothes from his wardrobe and his tools from the carport while we were all out at sport one Saturday. On arriving home you, Jamie, Megan and I stepped into the house together with a sense of foreboding and walked to the main bedroom as a tight group. We peered into the depth of Garth's wardrobe, at the bare shelves and the empty coat hangers. We stared, silent, bereft, abandoned. I had a knot in my stomach.

Then, you spotted something at the back of the lowest shelf and said in a bright voice, 'Bags his Noddy boots.' We looked at each other and laughed—you using your nickname for Garth's red boots. Your sense of humour melted an icy moment. We still laugh about it, despite the sadness.

The next shock came when your dad told me that he needed to sell our Wahroonga house "ASAP". Stunned by this, asked him where the children and I would live. He just shrugged. I saw a potential change of house and school at this stage as a massive disruption to our lives and sense of security. We had moved around so much already.

Garth went to a solicitor, but I said that because we had always worked things out together, why couldn't we now? We had both worked hard for our assets, so a fair distribution was paramount. I also knew that the children and

I being turfed out of the family home under these circumstances wasn't right.

With my accounting training, I put all our finances on the table and studied how I could keep the Wahroonga house, and pay the mortgage attached to it, leaving Garth with everything else, including 1 Sunset Boulevarde, for him to sell. There was no way I could keep the Eimeo house too, and stay put, so I apologised to you, Robbie, that I'd broken my promises that we would never sell our house on the beach in North Queensland, and that one day we would return. You nodded.

I experienced ongoing aggressive, nagging thoughts especially at night after dinner, when you kids had all gone to your rooms to do your homework. I needed to be calmer to think clearly, so I would often leave the house and walk around the quiet streets of Wahroonga with the dog until finally I felt more at peace.

One night I set out angry and troubled. I walked and walked and walked, and didn't get home till after ten. You came down the stairs quietly and asked gently if I was okay, then added, 'Have you rung Beverley today?' I was touched by your concern and said that walking had made me calmer and please, not to worry. I hadn't realised you'd been aware I'd left the house, or that you recognised how much my friend was helping. Even so, it was a long time before the shock and grief of Garth's departure diminished.

One Saturday, I walked with your dad out to the back gate as he was leaving after visiting you, Jamie and Megan. He looked at me gently and tenderly touched my cheek.

'You don't deserve this,' he said quietly. I wish he'd added that you and Jamie and Megan didn't deserve this either, but he turned and walked to the car.

I thought of the many times I had dreamed of our life together after he eventually retired from his all-consuming work. We would travel again, carefree, on adventures, as we had at the beginning. Your dad would make me laugh. We'd both be happy, sharing old and new experiences. But that was not to be.

NEVER TOO LATE TO TELL

* * *

On a walk to the park with our dogs, I confided in Kay that I wondered if Garth was leaving because I hadn't loved him enough and now it was too late? She said that it was never too late to love the qualities I appreciated about him. This thinking helped free me from resentful ruminating, although it did not happen immediately.

Years later, I discovered the American poet Sharon Olds' poem, '*Last look*', about the end of her thirty-year marriage. It seems to perfectly capture the appreciation I'd had for my marriage and my sadness at its demise.

> '*And I saw, again, how blessed my life has been,*
> *first, to have been able to love,*
> *then, to have the parting now behind me,*
> *and not to have lost him when the kids were young,*
> *and the kids now not at all to have lost him,*
> *and not to have lost him when he loved me, and not to have*
> *lost someone who could have loved me for life.*'

32

Bereft but Not Broken

It was wonderful having you living at home. Your presence and your music filled the house. Guns N' Roses boomed from upstairs. You taught me the lyrics of Axl's songs, 'Patience', 'Sweet Child O' Mine' and 'Welcome to the Jungle'. You played other rock bands like AC/DC but less often. Your favourite TV programme was Rage on ABC at the weekends. Sometimes we laughed together watching The Goodies and Monty Python.

On Friday mornings the whole house shook as you deliberately clomped heavily in cadet boots down the circular metal stairs. You'd appear in the kitchen resplendent in your tartan kilt and asked if I could drive you to school. You were keen on catching the bus every morning except Fridays when wearing the beautiful kilt. Usually, you would make sandwiches for your lunch before eating Weet-Bix with Jamie and Megan. A game of who smiles or blinks first, couldn't ever stop me from laughing however hard I tried to keep a serious facial expression or my eyes wide open.

You helped us all so much after your dad left, a time that I found so challenging. Your thoughtfulness included us in many ways. Before this I might have said, 'Would you like to empty the dishwasher?' 'No,' you would say. 'I wouldn't like to, but I will.'

Now you emptied the dishwasher without being asked, or mentioning it.

But you loved annoying me by spinning a bowl or saucepan lid like a top so it made a loud clattering noise twirling around on the bench or floor until coming to a shuddering stop.

You helped Jamie and Megan with their homework. As soon as you could drive, you drove Jamie to rugby practice or Megan to gymnastics classes or wherever else they wanted to go. I couldn't have asked for more consistent support.

I was determined to do everything I could to make you all feel secure, safe and loved. I wanted above all to help you develop into emotionally confident, independent adults. Other parents I met moaned about their wayward teenage sons and daughters, but in our family that was never true.

Kay invited us to a youth adventure camp being held at Little River, a tributary of the Hawkesbury River, near Wisemans Ferry, only an hour's drive away. You were definitely not interested in going. Kay was persuasive, and I was needing to gather us up to experience life as a whole family, so urged you to reconsider. Because I said how important it was to me that we all go together, you and Jamie agreed to come for the first two days of the five-day camp, as you already had plans with friends for the last few days of holidays.

So with this compromise we drove there. You were gloomy about the prospect of mixing with a whole bunch of complete strangers but within an hour of arriving at the camp, you and Jamie and Megan were caught up in the outdoor activities of abseiling, canoeing, tug of war and making friends.

When I saw you next at dinnertime you looked relaxed and were chatting to others your age.

After dinner there was a concert and games. I have a photo of you and Jamie doing handstands on the stage as part of your performance, and you doing a magic trick with one of the other boys your age. Megan enjoyed the activities with her friends.

The days you'd agreed to come went quickly. A photo taken just before you and Jamie left to return to Wahroonga by train from the Woy Woy Wharf shows you surrounded by your new companions who all said they wished you wouldn't leave. Effortlessly you had drawn these kids towards you.

I was so grateful that you had agreed to the Easter camp even though you hadn't wanted to go, that I planned a short trip for the next holidays. We drove to Fraser Island. Remember how you and Jamie had to dig the Subaru out when it got bogged in the sand numerous times? Someone told us to let the pressure down in the tyres to lessen the chance of being bogged, so you did. We saw photos of big four-wheel drive vehicles marooned in wet sand when they were caught by the incoming tide. We saw dingoes watching us around our tent.

Back at Wahroonga, we returned to work and school. You, Jamie and Megan all led busy and happy lives with friends and sport. You and Jamie worked on some weekends to earn money to buy any 'extras' you wanted.

Then in the holidays straight after you got your licence to drive on Ls I suggested a more adventurous trip as you could now share the driving. Your dad had always initiated far off car trips to unfamiliar places. He had made sure the petrol tank was full, the tyres pumped, and the car packed. If anything went wrong, he would fix it. But now you children concurred that there was no reason we couldn't take a long car trip without him. Woo hoo. Let's go! And grinning, we high-fived each other around the table.

* * *

Once again, Grandma and Grandpa agreed to drive up to Wahroonga from Melbourne to look after Buster and the garden while we were away. Grandma looked a bit worried as she watched me run up and down the stairs fetching towels and blankets, then filling boxes with packets of Weet-Bix, tins of biscuits, and baked beans and tuna from the pantry. I had worked until late at the office, then rushed home to prepare. She didn't think you children were pulling your weight, but then you packed the stuff neatly into the back of our station wagon.

I felt such a sense of excitement to be going on a carefree holiday with my three precious children that I was just happy to busily get ready for an early getaway in the morning.

We told Grandma and Grandpa we'd be back within three weeks and not to worry if they didn't hear from us while we were away. We had no set itinerary but were heading towards Uluru, which we at the time called Ayers Rock. I wonder what the highlights were of this adventure for you, Robbie? This is some of what I remember.

* * *

The large paper map stretched out in front of you, you deliberately rustled annoyingly as you folded a section over, to navigate the route. I suggested to Jamie that he write a journal of the trip, and include sketches of scenes, animals and people along the way.

'Should I draw every dead animal we see?' he asked. There certainly was a lot of roadkill on the verge. I forget just how many kangaroos, cows and birds we saw killed, but I can check Jamie's journal for detail.

I drove for eleven hours the first day, lighthearted, feeling like we'd escaped from oppression to freedom. We were all excited to be together on the road again, heading for new places and crossing borders into South Australia and the Northern Territory.

The first night, we pulled into the deserted Wilcannia caravan park and decided on an area overlooking the Darling River for you and the others to pitch the two tents. Then you collected firewood and got the fire going to cook chops. There wasn't a breath of wind, just quietness. I couldn't stop smiling. I was starting to unwind after a hectic few weeks at work preparing to take this time off.

In the morning we awoke to a soft mist rising from the river. It looked serene and I wished I was a poet to capture it.

With your new L-plates attached you wanted to drive the next day. I readily agreed, knowing that you would know the rules, like a slower maximum speed limit. It meant that as the only qualified driver I had to be the front seat passenger. Jamie and Megan would have to stay in the back.

Before starting the car you looked at the petrol gauge and said it was showing empty so drove back to the only garage in town. The petrol pump was chained up so I went into the shop and was given the key to unlock the chain. You filled the tank and I took the key back and paid the taciturn man behind the counter. The chained bowser was an indication of a troubled neighbourhood, but we had been blessed with a peaceful night.

We hadn't driven in desert-like areas in Australia before. The silvery saltbush, the only obvious vegetation, stood in stark contrast to the intense ochre colour of the earth. The saltbush had a distinctive smell in the dryness.

After ten hours of driving and much discussion we arrived in the South Australian industrial steel town of Port Augusta. As it was late and dark, do you remember, you drove into the first caravan park lit up?

Jamie decided to sleep in the car. The next morning we discovered that one of the car's tyres had been slashed. You and Jamie put on the spare. I was impressed at how easily you managed to do this and grateful for your confidence in removing and replacing a tyre for the first time. I knew at some point the slashed tyre would have to be mended but put it off for now.

After another full day travelling into ever-changing and increasingly barren country we decided against the caravan park at Glendambo, instead opting to pitch our tents out on an open stretch of ground away from the road.

Megan and I were sound asleep when we awoke to Jamie's shouting at us to get up.

'Why, what's the matter? What time is it? Can't it wait?' I said, snuggling further into my sleeping bag.

'No, we have to leave now,' Jamie said. 'Rob's and my tent is leaking and there's a puddle on the floor. We're packing our gear into the car. Hurry up, it's pouring, it's freezing and we're wet through.'

Grumbling, I complained that it was 5 am, and slowly joined the boys. You packed up Megan's and my tent with her help and threw our dripping stuff in the car. Everything was sopping, including us, but the heater soon warmed us.

When we spotted a fence on the outskirts of the next town that would be perfect to hang our gear on, we left it to dry in the strong wind and trusted that it would be there when we returned.

At Coober Pedy we found a cafe to have breakfast. After toast, bacon and eggs and a hot drink we felt much better. The underground house we were invited to look through had a modern kitchen and comfortable lounge. Its biggest advantage would be a constant temperature in contrast to outside where it was extreme. We were fascinated by this architecture, though I couldn't imagine living long term without windows, or greenery outside.

At the supermarket where we stocked up on supplies, we saw the widest variety of shoppers imaginable. There were rough-looking tradesmen, scruffy men and women of different nationalities, who I guessed were opal miners, and in contrast, elegantly dressed men and women, also a mixture of nationalities. Someone told us that anyone escaping from the law, or a marriage, or a lender, or an enemy of any kind could come to Coober Pedy, and blend in, no questions asked.

None of us could forget how you ignored the speed limits for L-platers—eighty kilometres per hour—when you overtook the road trains with fierce determination, thundering past the seemingly never-ending vehicle on a road that would not allow for another vehicle to pass. Us passengers sat leaning forward, anxiously holding our collective breath, only relaxing back in relief when we were on the left-hand side of the road again.

The first time, we all expressed amazement that a vehicle on the road could be so long. The second time, I think you took it as a challenge. Then I said not to do that again as the road trains roared along at astonishing speeds for vehicles so long, and our speed spiked to 120 kilometres an hour when passing them.

Apart from those moments, I thanked you for driving.

* * *

Alice Springs, which was hot and dusty, was our home for the next few days. We found a tyre place to fix the damaged one and did the short trip to Standley Chasm, a beautiful crystalclear river that had cut its way through the red rock over millions of years. While we stood there admiring the scene my hat blew off and sat up high on the water. There is a photo of us seemingly mesmerised, watching the hat gently floating off out of arm's reach before it disappeared around a bend. I wasn't amused, but you and the others thought it was hilarious.

Another day you took the Larapinta Drive, 131 kilometres to Hermannsburg. It seemed deserted as we wandered around looking at the buildings that had made up the Lutheran Mission from the 1890s to 1982. From there we headed for Palm Valley on a rough road and saw red cabbage palms in the only place they grow naturally.

After our days in Alice, with the spare tyre back in the boot, we headed for Ayers Rock. When we arrived at the campground, hopping mice were everywhere, but we managed to keep them out of the tents.

The next morning we drove to the rock and you and Jamie raced each other to the top, doing it in less than twenty minutes. Is that a record? You waited at the top for Megan who had walked next to me initially, but then continued when I stopped halfway up.

My main job was to photograph your climb using Rex's eight-millimetre movie camera. I moved a dial, thinking to capture close-ups, but unwittingly only photographed from the knees down. Jamie has reminded me that the result was like a Charlie Chaplin movie which when speeded up showed only quick feet movements. But none of you children were amused.

We drove the four hours from Uluru to Kings Canyon, after someone had told us it was well worth a visit. The steep sandstone walls rising about a hundred metres and the King River flowing along the bottom were a dramatic sight, with tall ghost gums growing along the banks. The rugged gorge, rocky domes and palm-fringed water holes were unexpected and beautiful.

After scoping the area, you and Jamie and Megan chose an open spot for a campsite with a few bushes and small trees nearby. You three set up camp, spread out pillows and sleeping bags in our tents, and organised a fire ready to cook dinner later.

Then you sat on a camp stool and were immediately engrossed in reading another book. Your concentration when reading, blocked out Megan and Jamie's throwing a ball to each other nearby, and me talking to them. The bag you packed for this trip consisted of spare undies, one T-shirt, a pair of shorts, a jumper, a toothbrush and seven books. You read all those books during that trip. The rest of us had brought one each. We walked up to the cliff's edge and along tracks, and stayed several nights.

After nearly three weeks of you doing most of the driving, and with Jamie and Megan helping to do most of the campsite setting up, we reluctantly headed for Wahroonga.

We loved having Grandma and Grandpa at home when we arrived back. Buster grinned and his tail didn't stop wagging.

* * *

For your sixteenth birthday, you had suggested to your dad and me that your preferred gift, if any, would be money for climbing gear. At the end of our street, Cliff Avenue, climbers had embedded metal bolts in the rocks which anchored ropes to use for rock climbing.

'Want to go abseiling, Mum?' you asked me one day.

'No, Robbie, definitely not,' I answered.

But you were persuasive and after months of you asking me, I agreed.

Obviously, you know all this Robbie, but I'll tell what it was like for me that day. Although I was reluctant, I was touched that you, my sixteen-year-old son, had invited me to share one of your favourite activities.

The morning of the abseil I found myself going to the toilet umpteen times, terrified at the thought of trusting in only a rope to keep me from falling.

Despite my misgivings, I trusted that you would never ask me, or anyone else, to do something dangerous. And you had tested the ropes down at the cliffs many times. You didn't consider this a dangerous activity.

I thought of the poster adorning your bedroom wall showing a climber hanging by one finger from a rock face at Chamonix.

'What's he doing?' I had asked you, puzzled.

'Strengthening the muscles in his fingers,' you explained.

* * *

Your strong hands pulled the straps of my climbing harness tight. I was wearing thick trousers tucked into socks and sturdy shoes, as you advised. I wanted to go to the toilet again but, of course, I couldn't now.

'That feels tight,' I said.

'Yes, it has to be,' you replied.

You did up the buckles, your hands steady, confident. I tried to listen.

'Hang on to the rope firmly behind you and lean back, your feet flat on the rock face as you walk down,' you said. 'You'll enjoy this, Mum.'

Enjoy? I didn't think so. Just let me survive, I thought. A rope passing through the descending device was attached to my harness by a carabiner.

Hesitatingly, I went to step off the cliff edge backwards, shaking, both hands gripping the rope.

'Don't look down,' you said.

I stopped. 'I can't do it, sorry.' I was nearly bawling.

'Yes, you can,' you said gently but firmly, and then I walked into space.

You urged me, encouraged me. 'You're okay, the rope's got you, you can't fall, you're safe.' My feet swung out alarmingly. Will this rope hold? Then I hit the cliff again. I gripped the rope even harder, then one foot found a narrow slit and the other firmed on a small ledge.

Your voice reached down to me. 'You're doing well, keep going, find another crack, there's a space for your left foot just to your left, a bit further, another few centimetres. No need for your fingers to grip, the rope's got you, lean back, you can't fall, you're safe.'

My foot dug into a cold, hard, shallow groove. I leant out, more confident, no longer wanting to hug the rock face.

'You're doing well, you're halfway down,' you called.

Bolder steps, until my feet touched... What's this? Solid ground.

Your friend, Richard, said, 'Well done.' I hadn't even been aware of him belaying at the bottom of the cliff.

Richard undid the rope connected to my waist via the clifftop anchors and removed it. I started laughing and was suddenly impatient to get back up to the top. Liberated, I bounded up the rocks at the side.

'Gosh, that was fun,' I said. 'Thanks, Robbie. Is there time for another go?'

* * *

Your climbing passion extended to climbing the Sydney Harbour Bridge at night, and this worried me when you finally told me about it. You had already done several climbs from different approaches and you described the evening when a friend begged to go with you. Your old canvas bag had accidentally dropped into the water. Your friend said to leave it. Surely it wasn't worth a plunge into the cold, dark, murky water under the bridge? But you, determined not to lose the bag, dived in, retrieved it, then swam to shore. What was that plunge like? Were you afraid of what was lurking in the dark water? Was the distance to the shore further than you'd realised? Did you consider sharks?

When you weren't down at the cliffs, you spent every day possible surfing at Warriewood or Mona Vale or another one of the Northern Beaches. Then one Saturday, Jamie came home from the beach early.

The following, Robbie, is the conversation Jamie and I had when he described how you had taught him to jump off the cliffs at the Warriewood Blowhole.

'How many metres down is the jump?' I asked.

'Not sure, but my shorts half tore off with the impact,' Jamie said. 'It's pretty scary looking down from the ledge in the howling wind.'

'Why did you do it?'

'I dunno, maybe 'cos Rob's mates were doing it? Rob's worked out a safe way to do it, scientifically, but it's still scary. We jump on the lump of a swell. He jumped first to test today's conditions. If they are ever not right, he doesn't do it.'

'What's it like landing in the water from that height?'

'The waves swept in, and then they took me out. It's hard not to try to fight the strong suck and swirl of the water. I swam forward as hard as I could a few metres and then I was pulled back a couple. I was aiming for the tunnel.'

'What's it like in the tunnel?'

'The tunnel's roof is high above you and dripping water, and the sides foam with the edges of swells, and the leftover waves hit the cliff. I swam forward, then got sucked back, swam ahead, got sucked back. Rob was in there with me enjoying it. I was glad he was there, but I was desperately looking for a way out. Rob was yelling at me. It was hard to hear over the echo and the crash of the waves. He kept yelling, 'Don't touch the sides.' There were razor-sharp shells there. Touch them and be cut to pieces, I realised.'

'How did you get out?'

'There's a rocky shelf that's only above sea level when the tide is low enough. There's a well there, maybe three metres deep, that fills and empties when the swell comes through the tunnel. I couldn't touch the bottom. All I wanted to do was to get out as fast as possible, but I had to be patient. I treaded water furiously and just waited in the white water. It was like being in a washing machine.

I waited for a surge of water big enough to fill the hole, then swam for the side and grabbed hold as fast as I could. The water level drops as fast as it rises. After a couple of attempts, I got out, clinging to a rock covered in slippery weed, with the receding water dragging at me. The blowhole drops to half its volume. A chasm opens up below you.'

'It sounds terrifying.'

'Yeah, it's scary, but Rob has worked out exactly what the sea, tides and waves should look like before the jump and how to think while navigating the tunnel without being cut to bits and getting out off the ledge without drowning. Yeah, it's scary physically, but it's even more of a mental challenge. I don't know how many people would find it fun, but Rob does.'

* * *

Jamie always looked up to you, Robbie, and trusted you, just as Megan and I did. You treated life as an unlimited adventure and others enjoyed sharing it with you. I wish I'd asked whether you were scared the first time you jumped off that cliff and negotiated the turbulent water below.

But, I have wondered since about your risky behaviour during those few years. I think back to your days of roaming around without supervision as a seven- and eight-year-old at Eimeo. You were more an adventurer than a risk-taker. I wonder if you were testing boundaries for what's possible?

I'm sure like most boys, you expected to continue enjoying life to the fullest through dangerous encounters. Healthy young people who live in a peaceful environment don't expect to die.

Your sudden plunge of interest in schoolwork was obvious. I put that down to you taking on the role of the man about the house, looking after all of us, which left little time for study.

I appreciate how much you did to ease the changes for me and Jamie and Megan. It was like a gaping hole had been ripped in the family fabric and you generously and thoughtfully assumed the role of filling it as much as you could.

Of course I was concerned that you never settled down to homework after school now. You often phoned from your friend Hugh's house to say that his mother had invited you to stay for dinner. Later, you told me that you spent hours after school sitting with Hugh and his older sister Sarah in their spa.

Diminutive and blonde with startling blue eyes and a lovely speaking voice, Sarah endeared us to her the minute you brought her home to meet us.

The first time I saw her, you and she were sitting on the couch in our living room, your arm draped over her shoulders. If she visited when you were down at the park playing tip footy with the others, Sarah would put her arm around Megan, and they'd walk off together and go to watch. When she came to our place for meals there was a lot of laughter, but more often you would eat at her family's home in Warrawee.

Sarah was polite, easy to talk to, and interested in our stories of the places and lifestyles we'd experienced. She was obviously very fond of you.

33

You Are the Best Thing

I came home from your Year 12 parent-teacher night, my head spinning with the negative feedback of your teachers. You were always in the top stream for every one of your subjects, but your position in those classes had dropped dramatically. All your teachers were gloomily pessimistic.

'Unfortunately Robert has left it too late to reverse his downward spiral so close to the finals,' they said. 'Other students have been studying hard for nearly two years by this stage, aware that they are vying for selective placements at university.'

Some of your results at the trial exams had been dismal and those marks counted towards your final score. The marks in your final exams would count for more, but how much difference could studying in the last few weeks make?

I put on my disappointed voice when relaying to you what your teachers had said, but of course I wasn't disappointed in you. Overnight you had assumed the role of caring for me and your siblings. Other things were more relevant to you now than schoolwork.

You were a wonderful individual, working hard at being a good son, brother, friend, and being yourself. You were holding down a part-time job at the service station, and you had a lovely relationship with Sarah. What were exams compared to that?

Nevertheless, I did wonder if there was anything I could do to reverse your lacklustre attitude to schoolwork just for these last few weeks.

On her most recent visit, Grandma had been worried too.

'He's not studying,' she had said. 'Shouldn't he be studying?'

'Yes, Mum, he should.' I had said. Was it too late?

I wanted to show you how serious I was about wanting you to do better. I offered you a monetary reward for making a last-ditch effort. I said you could think that I was paying you to do a job. You accepted. You locked yourself in your room for the entire two weeks before the finals. You lost that perpetual restlessness that previously had you gathering your climbing ropes for an abseil or climb at the local cliffs. You spent less time gazing into the fridge too and walking away empty-handed.

During these weeks I often asked Megan to tell you that dinner was ready. She came downstairs and described how your elbows were resting on the desk, your head in your hands, which were twined through your matted hair, staring down at your papers. Apparently, you took a while to register that she was at the door and slowly turned to look at her as though dazed.

'Rob's in another world,' she said. 'It took him a while to recognise me.'

I saw this same concentration when you wandered down the stairs one day and I asked what you were studying. 'A four unit maths problem,' you replied, adding, 'I've been working on it since yesterday.'

Aware of how few days you had to cover all thirteen subject units I said, 'Shouldn't you just drop that and get on with chemistry or French?'

You just stared at me as though through a pea souper fog and went slowly back upstairs. Later you appeared looking relieved and said you'd solved it.

You never reacted to my worried nagging, just held your ground and did what you had in mind.

Your HSC results rebuffed the sceptics. As you know, those two weeks of deeply focused concentration got you through French, English, chemistry and physics, as well as three and four unit maths—the latter being a subject offered by only some schools to the brightest students. Your score for it was ninety-seven per cent.

When you came home from work and opened that envelope and read your results, the relief and happiness on your face were beautiful to see.

I gave you a big hug. 'You deserve this success,' I said. 'I'll phone Grandma. She will be delighted too.'

Then you headed off to share the news with your friends and Sarah. I wonder what she had already told you about uni life in the hours you spent with her and Hugh, sitting in their home spa?

You pored over the list of courses offered at the University of Sydney and rejected one after the other. Architecture, archaeology, engineering and science sparked at least some interest. You settled on combining science and engineering degrees, then decided to defer for a year to work full time at the service station, earn some money and apply for the Chancellor's Scholarship next year.

Your boss was planning to work less and let you take over as manager. It meant more interesting work and more money. After those summer holidays, Megan and Jamie returned to school and I took two months' leave without pay to trial a job working from home. You used to ride your bike every day from the service station to have lunch with me.

During those few weeks I enjoyed just the two of us having an hour together in the middle of the day. It was one of the most precious periods of my life. We talked like old friends. You described customers' peculiar behaviour that made me laugh, and your boss's plans for his future. You asked if I thought it mattered that Sarah was older than you. Of course not, I'd said. Garth was younger than me.

One day you stood up from the table to leave and on impulse I stood too, reached my arms around you and gave you a long hug.

'You are the best thing that has ever happened to me,' I said.

I have thought since about how glad I am to have told you that, how spontaneous, and how true.

Then your boss changed his mind, and you decided that you would like to go to uni that year after all. You wrote to the Dean of Engineering asking if you could start now, even though the academic year had already begun several weeks before. No, he replied, the students in the course had already learnt too much and you would never catch up. You wrote again, emphasising your HSC maths and physics results, and were allowed to begin. You quickly caught up with the subjects already covered. There was even a welding session which you really enjoyed. I suppose your previous experience of welding at Bill's farm had given you a head start in that skill.

I was relieved that you were revelling in the freedom and interests that university life was offering. You were settled, happy and bursting with life.

Then one afternoon, on your way home from uni with friends, six weeks after you'd started, the unthinkable happened. A freak accident, police and individuals said. Others said to me, 'Hasn't everyone casually leant back out the open door of a red rattler?'

What occurred made no sense. You could scale cliffs and leap into blowholes and always return home safely. You had such a knowledge of physics, so much common sense. Maybe you had been daydreaming about the design you were planning to paint on the T-shirts you would sell?

But that afternoon in the tunnel between Wynyard and Milsons Point Stations, you decided unthinkingly or dreamily to try leaning back out of the open door of a crowded Sydney red rattler after friends had told you what fun it was when they had done it. As you casually leant back the protruding signal box was precisely at your head height in that split second.

Two other trains sped through the tunnel, their drivers oblivious of a body next to the tracks. Then they closed the North Shore Line. Commuters were left standing around on the stations, waiting for trains to reappear. It was on the evening news.

Richard told me that the friends who had been travelling in the carriage with you were questioned. Questions about what your behaviour was like, and your demeanour before you leant back? You had been happily talking and laughing, they said. The police would send this information from eyewitnesses to the coroner.

Weeks later I caught the train to Central Station and attended the NSW Registry of Births, Deaths and Marriages to read the coroner's report and sight the death certificate. The coroner had determined and written—death by accident. I did not purchase a copy of the certificate.

I knew when you left home that morning you had been happy, healthy and bursting with youthful energy. You were on the cusp of enjoying everything about life going forward.

I was and am confident that as you adventured on into a new experience, your intelligence, humour, strength and love for others would continue to be a blessing. Those qualities make up your eternal identity in my consciousness. But it has taken me decades to realise that so confidently.

*   *   *

In the days and weeks after the phone call Richard made to me from Milsons Point Station I struggled to process what had happened. Everything felt surreal. But you filled my thoughts.

Were you okay? I reached out to you mentally knowing you were spiritually alive, but with no concept of your current experience. I recalled over and over my last minutes with you at the back gate at Wahroonga and later hearing your reassuring voice in the morgue. How glad I was to have told you that you were the best thing that had ever happened to me. I'm so glad you heard me say that, Robbie, and you still are.

34

Surreal Days

Robbie, I'll tell you how each of the first few days at Wahroonga passed, after you had left.

Day One. I was conscious of your presence. I felt that you needed me to keep you consciously in my thoughts in case you needed my support. As a child in new situations, if you were ever shy, nervous or afraid, I would be there to comfort and reassure you. Now, although I couldn't know in human terms what you were experiencing, I felt impelled to metaphorically hold your hand, as I felt you were holding mine.

This focus allowed no space for an outpouring of grief. Also, I was feeling intense gratitude for your presence in my life for eighteen years. I think this protected me from overwhelming despair, but also I was still in shock. It didn't mean sadness wasn't present, just that initially concentrating on you was more pressing.

I did need hands-on help. I phoned Bill and Betsy. Your Uncle Bill said he would arrange for someone to care for his animals and make the two-flight trip down to Sydney within days. Betsy, my oldest friend, now a GP in Melbourne, similarly said she would find a way to leave her medical practice and fly up to be with me.

Betsy and I rode our bikes to high school together nearly every day, chose the same subjects, and sat together in class. We shared our first parties and had remained friends over the years throughout my many moves.

You might not remember, but as a toddler you had stayed with Betsy and Chester a few times when your dad and I attended company-organised weekend-away do's. I needed her understanding and support now.

Day Two. I phoned Grandpa to wish him a happy birthday, then told him the devastating news. Grandpa went quiet, then said he'd go and tell Grandma. Grandma came to the phone and spoke in a soft trembling voice. I said I'd phone them again later. I felt so sad for them. They needed a huge hug. I went to the Rocks Police Station for the second time and then visited the morgue, where I shared your physical presence for the last time.

At home the atmosphere was too surreal for Jamie and Megan to go to school. They were quiet when I left. Pam was coming to be with them again.

That evening a group of your close friends joined Jamie and Megan in our lounge room and I talked to them about my strong sense that your life was continuing. I don't know if what I said was meaningful to them, but they left looking less distraught.

Day Three. Jamie and Megan chose to return to school, so the house was silent. The telephone had stopped ringing. I roused myself to mundane tasks. I needed to make phone calls to people about arrangements, to say thank you to others, and return calls that had gone to the answering machine earlier. I made a list of them all and dialled the number at the top. No-one answered. I phoned the next number to which there was no answer. After trying five numbers with no response, I realised that this was not what I should be doing right then.

I stopped planning. My instinct told me to sit quietly. When I argued that I should be getting on, that inner voice was gentle, persistent.

I wandered to the couch in the lounge room and gazed out the double glass doors. It was a mild and sunny May day outside, and the bougainvillea was flowering deep red along the back fence. My thoughts became still. A sense of peace engulfed me as my eyes drifted to the clear blue sky. My consciousness lifted. It soared as I saw a soft-edged shaft of intensely bright light lifting upwards and I knew you were part of it. I felt intense love engulfing us both.

Before this, I had felt closer to you, Robbie, than any other human, but we were always separate individuals with the potential to drift apart as humans might. But then, with my epiphany on the couch that day, I knew that in my consciousness, we couldn't be separated.

* * *

Bill arrived and took to answering the phone. Betsy spoke to people at the door, taking delivery of soups, casseroles, cakes, cheese platters and flowers.

Kind and generous friends, neighbours and strangers, friends of you, Jamie and Megan were bringing gifts. The house seemed magically filled with the perfume of lilies, roses, freesias, peonies and carnations. Betsy scrambled to find enough vases to hold them. Pots bursting with cyclamens, red, pink and white, were placed around the rooms.

When I walked through the florist-like lounge and dining rooms from my bedroom to the kitchen I felt comforted. The beautiful flowers symbolised to me, expressions of love, of compassion, kindness and empathy.

Betsy talked gently to Megan and Jamie and prepared meals for us all. Bill and Betsy's help allowed me the space to be still, to feel connected to you, as you ventured into the unknown. My bedroom became my sanctuary where I remained for hours undisturbed.

Dr Paterson, the headmaster, phoned and suggested we use the Knox Grammar School chapel for a memorial service. He also offered to write and deliver the eulogy. I asked the chaplain, Reverend Godfrey, if I could prepare the service. Apparently, it was an unusual request but he graciously agreed.

The school needed a date as soon as possible which was difficult to set because I couldn't reach your dad. I had to assume he would be back at work on Monday as his colleague had predicted, so we set a date for your memorial service to be the day after.

Day Four. Betsy and I read and selected passages from the Bible that we liked and thought appropriate. We selected hymns from the Christian Science Hymnal that had beautiful words, and melodies that would be familiar to many people. I asked Richard, Hugh and Sarah if they would read scriptural selections. They bravely agreed. I sent the service details to the Knox office for printing.

Day Five. First thing, I phoned Garth at work hoping he had returned from holiday. He was there so I told him briefly what had happened and that we had booked the Knox chapel for the memorial service tomorrow. His voice was shaking when he said he would come to the service and would telephone Allie, Rex and Danny who were all living at Shoal Point in North Queensland. He hoped they could come at such short notice.

That night, your Uncle Kim arrived with Grandma and Grandpa from Melbourne, after a ten-hour drive.

I had not sought religion, but my next-door neighbour had introduced me to a deeply caring, simple teaching at the exact moment when I needed the most help. It gave me direction and strength and courage. Firstly, that was when I lost Garth, and now, when you were physically gone so suddenly.

Day Six. I woke up early on the morning of 7 May 1991. This was the day set to publicly celebrate your life.

Grandma had never let me go to funerals. She would never have thought that the first one I would ever attend would be my own son's and that he would be just eighteen.

I wondered if I had to attend and considered not going because I didn't feel brave enough to face other people. Would it matter? I had no energy for the expected outpouring of grief.

In funerals I'd seen on TV, the mother is always in black, wiping her eyes and weeping, with people on either side steadying her. But, I realised, others will need comforting today, so I should be there. Everyone would expect me to attend and of course I wanted to celebrate your life.

Now, I needed to get dressed.

I had never worn black, so I didn't have any black clothes. I stared into my wardrobe for something suitable, pushing the coat hangers to the side, one after the other. At the end was my best dress. It was Thai silk and a bright bluey-green. I would wear that.

When I finally left my bedroom, I found Grandma and Grandpa, Kim, Bill, Jamie and Megan already downstairs and sitting around the kitchen table all wearing their best clothes. Hugh had driven Bill to the local menswear outfitters to hire a suit for the occasion.

'Cup of tea?' Grandma asked me gently.

'No, thanks, Mum.'

We drove in two cars, the school only five minutes away. People were milling around on the lawn outside the chapel. Who were they all? I didn't recognise any of their faces.

Scaffolding around the building blocked the main entrance, so people were queued up, waiting to go in the side door. A prefect spotted Jamie. He ushered us in and led us, past pews already full, to the front one. Then a stream of boys from Jamie's year filed in, serious, respectful. The people last to arrive had to stand at the back.

Later, I discovered that about a hundred of those attending were boys in your year group along with their mothers. Those who heard about it too late rang the school for copies of the eulogy.

Following is most of what Dr Paterson said about you.

* * *

Robert came to see me only days ago to ask for a reference. He walked into my office, totally at ease, as the cloak of a schoolboy had fallen away completely and we spoke man-to-man.

The last time I'd spoken to Robert, I was telling him to straighten his tie, to please do something, anything about his hair, and to tuck in his shirt. I taught him in fifth form, where I found his unused natural ability frighteningly dormant.

So it was good to meet him like this, man-to-man, and to sense the special qualities that marked him, in those scriptural words we've heard this morning, as being "I am that I am". And it was something about him then that I sensed, for Robert would never tell about himself—you had to find out.

One of his close friends summed him up like this: Rob is always content. Forever relaxed and friendly, he is guided by a natural enthusiasm for friendship and fun, rather than materialistic gain.

Another said: Uninhibited and never bitter, he is a loyal and constant friend with a powerful zest for life that deeply touched everyone he met. One in a million.

And another: Everyone who has known Rob has benefited from knowing him. His friendship touched many.

And another: Being part of Rob's life has filled my life with so many good experiences, that Rob has taken a permanent place in my memory, a loveable guy, never to be forgotten.

And another: Rob loves us in a way that is good and strong and quiet. He taught me that you don't need words to care about someone heaps.

And another: Rob has no enemies. He made many good friends, and it is just wonderful to be one of them.

Rather powerful testimonies to this unusual guy. He was amazingly clever. In his early years at Knox, he walked away with scholastic prizes until schoolwork became less creative, dulled by the need to prepare for public examinations. So Robert stopped working. He took an arcane pleasure in walking out of his HSC Trials with three pins on his lapel, having written only single-page answers to examinations.

He projected to his peers that oozing strength and contentment that I sensed in my office recently, so they knew it all before I did. No boy was more at peace with himself and the world around him. He was an honest and sincere human being, without the slightest pretence. He infiltrated his contentment among others. If angered, it was over in a flash, smiting his momentary enemy with a winning smile.

As one of his good mates said, he was frustratingly good to everyone, even blokes we didn't like, he did.

And another close friend said: Rob is the best bloke I've ever met. No upfront, upstage fellow, Rob instead quietly infiltrated himself on those around him, whoever they were. His easy talk and ready banter, laced with his slang language and his sheer joy of life, instantly befriended him to all. You felt Robert's peace within himself, and you relaxed and felt good in his company. He exuded energy.

Another close friend recalled: To me, Rob is a guy who is high on life. He didn't need anything to help him enjoy what he already had. He ran on adrenaline and continuously looked for adventures. His naturally strong and well-coordinated body allowed him to tackle any sport or adventurous activity with ease. He climbed mountains, abseiled from heights, leapt into waters low below cliffs, and most of all, dazzled his friends at tip footy. He seemed indestructible, taking the wind in his face water and snow skiing, skateboarding, even boogie board skiing on water-laden tennis courts, and bicycling.

Robert was an artist and cartoonist. He would draw caricatures of teachers and sit in the front of the class, holding up the drawing to observe for himself the similarities between the teacher and the cartoon. Those classmates behind him were thoroughly entertained.

Robert did not drink, nor did he smoke. But, my goodness, he ate! That yellow satchel each day contained a pile of sandwiches, oranges and fruit. He enjoyed plain water, was the driver after parties, and his top drinks were Milo and iced coffee.

It is a tough world out there. "Welcome to the jungle", Robert might have echoed from his favourite Guns N' Roses song. Then he'd declare himself in complete command of his place in that jungle, creating for himself some openness and space which then magically filled with happy, relaxed people who so completely and unreservedly loved him as Robert loved them.

A real character, the one in a million, the bright star in the jungle, the fellow who shone his light of peace and love upon others, I am that I am.

It is my honour and pleasure to have been personally touched by Robert in that fleeting time in my office for he exuded peace and goodness and simplicity.

* * *

Those who were there listened spellbound as Dr Paterson spoke. Sometimes people laughed and at other times some cried. I was grateful for his words, and to those of good friends, like Pam, who shared with me the letter she wrote to our ex-neighbour Kay recounting the day.

> *'Like the surge of a wave streamed in beautiful people, the place filled with eternal youth. The chapel, by commencement time, was brimming over as people crowded to share this moment of life and light. In this service, no creed nor age separated us. We all seemed bound together in the radiance of life that permeated everything. Then the Headmaster stood to speak. As he began, there was a sense of joy, of life, of love, everywhere. I watched the young men sitting in the block of pews across from me as they visibly relaxed. They were with Rob, as Dr Paterson so expertly brought him before us in all his unique individuality. No longer was there shocked grief, instead only companioning with life.*
>
> *I must admit to tears at the beauty of the moment when one of Rob's friends played the Tribute on the bagpipes.*
>
> *Then, uplifted, we surged out onto the lawn. There, in a beautiful blue dress that shone was Meg, radiant, as she greeted each one of us.'*

As people filed out of the chapel into the sunshine, I stood inwardly numb but outwardly greeting people as they approached. I overheard two boys standing a little apart, disgruntled, saying, 'She hasn't even spoken to us, we needn't have come.' I turned around and recognised them as two boys you'd shared the boarding house with years before. I dredged up the strength to approach them. I spoke to them softly and thanked them for coming. They walked off subdued.

I caught some people staring at me, perhaps wondering to themselves what would they say? Some came up to me and said what a wonderful boy you were. Others, having heard Dr Paterson's eulogy, felt they knew you.

After the service many young people came back to our house, where an army of your and Jamie's friends' mothers had taken over the kitchen. These mothers made cups of tea and coffee and offered cakes and slices and scones.

Your uni friends, many of whom I hadn't met before, congregated at a table under the grapevine.

Your dad, Jamie, Megan and I sat together, not talking, just looking on from a bench near the bougainvillea.

Your dad was tearful. You shared so many of the qualities I had loved about Garth, especially the capacity to make me laugh. Although your dad hadn't been there when I first learned of your existence, nor when I heard of your accident, he was at your birth. By supporting us we then became a family. And now he was here, and he needed our support.

No-one seemed to expect me to say or do anything, everyone was just milling around, introducing themselves to each other and talking. For me, just being there was hard. I still couldn't think, except for the thought that I would be glad when everyone left, though I appreciated their condolences. I just wanted to be alone with you. Your presence was palpable, at least to me. Maybe others felt it too.

Day Seven. This day, the Reverend Godfrey conducted a service at the crematorium. Only immediate family members attended.

Your grandfather, Rex, and your uncle, Danny, who had both flown down from Mackay, joined us there. They had had too little notice to book flights in time for the Knox chapel service.

Rex said to me gently, 'I'm so sorry, Margaret, I know how proud you were of Rob.'

Afterwards, we all talked quietly under the pergola at home. It was the first time Rex had met Grandma and Grandpa. He came to me in the kitchen and said, 'Your parents are lovely, Margaret.'

Day Twenty-One. I suggested to Garth, Jamie and Megan that we have a picnic at Warriewood, overlooking the blowhole where you had spent so many afternoons jumping over the cliff. Your ashes could fly over as you had done, I suggested. Everyone agreed that you would rather have your ashes carried out by wind and tide than be buried somewhere.

On that Sunday afternoon, no-one else was there. We peered down at the turbulence below and wondered if you would have gauged the conditions conducive to a jump. I opened the lid of the box, and each of us threw a handful of fine grey dust into the air, intending for it to go out to sea. It blew straight back into our faces. As I picked ash out of the corner of my eyes, I said, smiling, 'Do you think he's letting us know he's still here?'

35

Your Inclusive Nature

You added so comprehensively to my life, Robbie. I find it hard to tell you in words how much. I get a surging sense of privilege for our shared eighteen years.

In this outline of when and where you came into the world, I am hoping that you recognise it as a story of love and gratitude.

There are times I dearly wish you and I could have a hug or a chat or share a book or a meal. I sometimes muse on what you might be doing here had you not left. On television, I see scientists who are also thrillseekers experimenting while doing seemingly dangerous things. Other scientists are working on rockets and space exploration. Maybe you would help address the threat of climate change? I see cartoonists bringing important and complex topics to light with a few pen strokes and insightful words. I see engineers inventing systems or designs for future constructions. I see young engineers from all over the world bring their solar-designed cars to compete in the three-thousand-kilometre race from Darwin to Adelaide. I see how easily you could have been any one of them.

In any of these pursuits you would have effortlessly drawn in those around you. Your inclusive nature was evident within minutes of your birth. You looked straight into the eyes of the six people in that labour ward, one after the other. Each one seemed important to you. Not one individual was left out of your steady gaze which instantly drew them towards you. You had only been minutes in this world. Your inclusive nature continued, and continues.

There are moments when I forget you are not here. Before I left Sydney to move to Wandiligong ten years ago I was driving past the house in Wahroonga. I slowed down and I grinned and I said, 'Look, Robbie, there's the triffid.'

When we first moved in, before we knew about gymea lilies one had suddenly appeared in our garden, its giant thick green stem so tall it looked as though it was going to reach the second floor of the house. At the top of it burst a huge bright red flower.

You and I had called it a triffid and always laughed. I glanced over at the passenger seat. It was empty, but I heard your soft chuckle.

May 2, 2021

Thirty years ago today you physically left us, Robbie. Three years ago I sat on the deck at Wandi and started telling you the story I had always wanted to tell you. Three months ago I contacted some of the people mentioned in our story to ask them if they were comfortable to be named. I enjoyed speaking with them after so many years and they were pleased to hear from me. I had wondered if your story should be shared with others. Their expression of love for you has encouraged me to do so.

I scanned my phone contacts and rang the only number listed that was connected to your old school friends, Rosalie, Jamie G's mother. She recounted that within the week after your accident, a group of your friends had gathered at their house one evening. They sat in a circle on the floor, quiet, sorrowful, comforting each other by being together. As she handed the boys cups of Milo she realised how much you meant to them all. 'Everyone loved Rob,' she said. She gave me her son Jamie's number.

Jamie G played the bagpipes at your memorial service in the Knox Chapel. He and I had a long chat. You would remember him from sharing many classes and he has continued to be in contact with other close friends, Hugh, Richard and Harry, so shared their numbers.

I found a photo of you cutting Harry's hair in the backyard of our Wahroonga house and texted a copy to him. I asked if he remembered that haircut. His reply was, 'Yes, I remember 100% this haircut. I have been thinking about Rob often lately.' You and he had a lot of fun together as boarders and when he came to Wahroonga for a weekend or you went to stay with his dad at Mudgee.

Hugh returned my text message by phoning me. We talked about the day you left and how difficult it was to think clearly on that day. He remembered Richard telephoning him from The Rocks Police Station (I didn't know that the boys had gone there too), and asked to be picked up. Richard, along with David B had been asked by the police to give witness statements because they were with you on the train. Hugh's memory of that night was hazy, but he thought several boys had come to their house that night, to comfort each other. I asked him for his sister Sarah's number.

When I phoned Sarah, she immediately recognised my voice, amazing after three decades. Her voice sounded pleasantly the same as I remembered too. She agreed with Hugh that your friends had gathered at their house that first night trying to make sense of what had happened. I read to her the sections where I included her as your girlfriend and asked if she was happy for that to be printed. She said, 'Yes.' I found a sweet photo in the album of a pretty Sarah helping Megan dress for a school formal.

Richard was on holidays in North Queensland when I spoke to him. We had an emotional, tender conversation after decades of no communication. He told me how much he had continued and continues to think about you. He told me that he, Harry and Jamie G cycle together, and you are often included in their conversations. 'Wouldn't Rob love to be here,' he said, they might say when stopping for a drink break on a long ride, or, 'Rob would love to do this.'

In reply to my query, Dr Paterson said that he'd be honoured to be in the book. It must have been on the third night when he generously and thoughtfully invited many of your friends to his house to share insights about you as their friend. He wrote your eulogy based on a recent meeting he'd had with you, you'd gone to his office for a reference, but mostly around what your friends told him that night.

It was wonderful to talk to Tricia Newman, recently. Still living near Tring, she knew you before your birth and as 'that beautiful baby at Arbour House'. Although decades had passed since we were in touch, Tricia and I spoke as though we were sitting in the garden having morning tea with Chris and your dad. We reminisced about how happy those days had been both before you were born, and after when, you, your dad and I became a family. Tricia was so supportive of us when we lived in the caravan in her garden. You were important in her life too, and she spoke of you with rich memories.

Love defined your life from the start, and nothing has stopped it reaching out to others. Thank you, Robbie.

Arbour House, England

Robbie's British passport photo 1972

Robbie asleep on a bench, Versailles, France

Robbie and Grandpa, Melbourne, Vic

Donga, Dysart, Qld

Jamie and Megan in bulldust, Dysart, Qld

Plettenberg Bay, South Africa

Hydroponics, Eimeo, Qld

Canoe in flood, Eimeo, Qld

Megan, Jamie, Robbie, Eimeo, Qld

Sunday lunch, Eimeo, Qld

Studying echidna, NSW

Robbie, picnic, Scone, NSW

Sue visits Scone, NSW

New bikes, Scone, NSW

Puppies, Scone, NSW

First day at Knox Grammar School, NSW

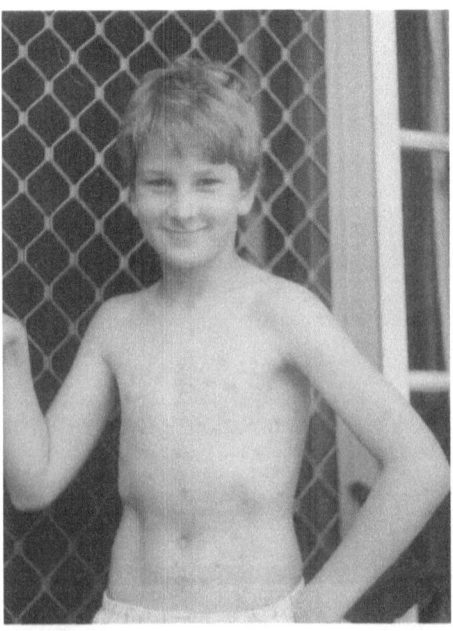

Matron's photo of Rob with measles at school hospital

Robbie, Year 11 school formal

Robbie at cliffs, Wahroonga, NSW

Robbie at cliffs, Wahroonga, NSW

Jamie, Robbie, Kings Canyon, NT

Robbie, Lake Boga, Vic

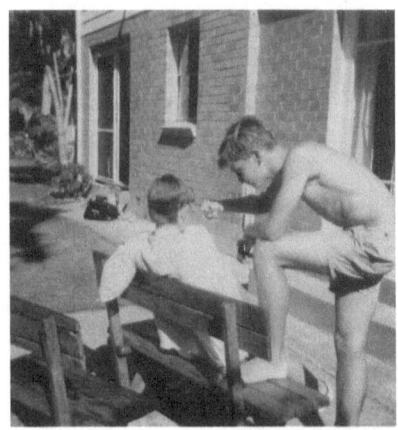

Harry's haircut, Wahroonga, NSW

Robbie, school formal, 1989

End year 12, Rob, Mum and Richard behind

Grandma, Robbie, Jamie, Dec 1990

Acknowledgements

Thank you Sue Hargreaves for friendship in fun adventures. I started writing this when we were together at Patti Miller's memoir class in Paris. In many of your phone calls from NZ, Sue, you urged me to not give up when I had had enough of writing.

Thanks Patti for your sensitive teaching in Paris, Sydney and Melbourne. I would not have embarked on this book without your interest and encouragement.

I am indebted to 'the writing whisperer' Dr Carol Major, for her advice on shaping the story, at Varuna, The National Writers House. Thank you, Carol.

And thank you Varuna for the opportunity to experience an atmosphere conducive to writing.

Anne Mainsbridge and I spent hours together sharing our early writing. Thank you Anne, for your feedback on my early pieces and for your companionship at writing festivals.

Thanks to Anthony Reeder and Louisa Costa who added editorial suggestions to original drafts.

Thanks to Liz Taylor, Judy Flanders and Marianne Dredge who read an early manuscript and responded with positive feedback.

Thank you Natasha Gilmour at the kind press for your professional guidance through the publishing process.

To Jim and Megan whose lives are weaved through this story too. Thank you for the insightful details you offered of the experiences we shared with Robbie.

About the Author

M. A. Hughes is a mother of three and a grandmother of three boys, who lives tranquilly on a hazelnut and chestnut farm in northeast Victoria. Nearly thirty years ago her firstborn son was killed at eighteen. She speaks directly to him through her first book, *Never Too Late to Tell*.

www.ingramcontent.com/pod-product-compliance
Lightning Source LLC
Chambersburg PA
CBHW021941290426
44108CB00012B/922